Four Square (4□) Writing Method

for Grades 7-9

Written by Judith S. Gould, Evan Jay Gould and Mary F. Burke

Illustrated by Christina D. Schofield
Cover Designed by Kati Baker

Teaching & Learning Company

a Lorenz company
P.O. Box 802
Dayton, OH 45401-0802
www.LorenzEducationalPress.com

D1567366

This book belongs to

_____

Acknowledgments

Thanks to the students, administration and staff of Windy Hill Elementary School and R.M. Paterson Elementary School for piloting the program and believing in it.

Thanks to Peter Correa and Barbara Najdzion for technical and artistic support.

About the Authors

Judith S. Gould

Judy is a teacher, writer and educational speaker who has been sharing ideas for writing success in schools nationwide. She has taught nearly all grades, including Pre-K and high school. When at home in Florida, she enjoys reading and writing with husband Evan, daughter Ilana and Figaro the cat.

Evan Jay Gould

Evan Gould has been teaching music and drama for over 10 years. He teaches at Paterson Elementary School in Florida where he has been named teacher of the year. He has had great success integrating the basic subject areas into his hands-on art program. He is currently enrolled at the University of Florida in a program for Educational Leadership in Administration.

Mary F. Burke

Mary has been a teacher for 23 years. She is currently the writing teacher at Jacksonville Beach Elementary in Florida. She enjoys writing poetry and having a simple life with her husband Cal and her dog, Mel and cat, Ripley.

Pictures © Corel Corporation

Copyright © 2010, Teaching & Learning Company

ISBN 978-1-4291-1743-2

Teaching & Learning Company • a Lorenz company • P.O. Box 802 • Dayton, OH 45401-0802

TLC10581

Table of Contents

How to Use This Book 5

Section 1: Getting Organized 6

Section 2: Other Forms of Composition 59

Section 3: Samples of Four Squares and Essays 74

Section 4: Four Square and Beyond 83

Section 5: Practice Prompts 100

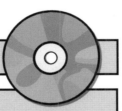

Pages Included on the Enhanced CD:

- Narrative, informational, descriptive, and persuasive Four Square plans and their accompanying written pieces

- Eight different partially-completed Four Square plans for students who need this particular kind of scaffolding

- Examples and instruction on how to lead your students to *extended elaboration*

- "How to Four Square" PowerPoint Presentation

Dear Teacher or Parent,

In collegiate studies of elementary education, future teachers learn about the importance of writing as a language art. Students of elementary education are told that it is a vital form of expression and a communication skill that is required of the workforce of the future. Writing is touted as an interdisciplinary link for classroom teachers to apply almost universally. Today's teachers are aware of the assessments that students will face, and that the basic language arts skills are vital to their success.

Even while writing has taken a stronger role in the schools, a gap has developed between primary and secondary levels. High school teachers are quick to point out that students arrive without the skills to take an essay test or to write a term paper. Yet elementary education teachers have difficulty in inspiring and simplifying the writing process for our fledgling students.

While this disparity has existed for a long time, it did not escalate to crisis proportion until states began assessing the writing of their elementary-age students. The results attest that too many of our children lack fundamental writing skills. Many cannot produce a focused, well-supported, and organized composition.

Why do we struggle with the teaching of writing? When we teach children to read, we give them decoding skills to use. When we teach science, we give them the scientific method. When we teach mathematics, we give them skills and drill specific facts. In writing, too, we need to provide specific skill instruction if we are to expect results.

In the following chapters, we present a method of teaching basic writing skills that is applicable across grade levels and curriculum areas. It can be applied to the narrative, descriptive, informational, and persuasive writing form. Prewriting and organizational skills will be taught through the use of a graphic organizer. This visual (and kinesthetic) aid is employed to focus writing, to provide detail, and to enhance word choice. It is an excellent aid in preparing students for the demand/prompt draft writing assessments being given throughout the country.

Teaching writing through the use of a graphic organizer empowers students to write with confidence. It facilitates whole group differentiation, providing students with a similar assignment and open-ended outcomes. The graphic organizer helps students to visualize the structure for a coherent delivery of ideas.

We hope you will use the Four Square to help your students have writing successes!

Sincerely,

Judith, Evan & Mary

Judy and Evan Jay Gould & Mary Burke

TLC10581

How to Use This Book

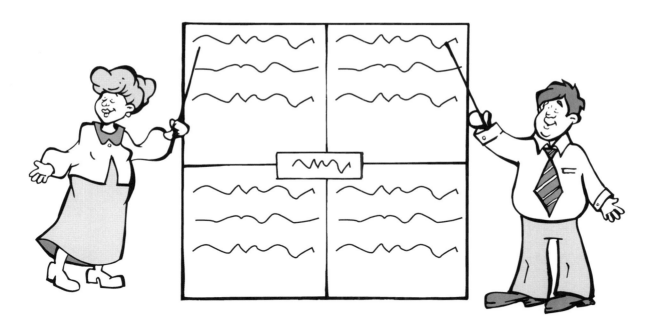

Four square instruction and practice should be incorporated into a writing program that is rich with writing experiences. During the learning of the organizer, students should maintain poetry, shared writing and journal writing activities.

Section 1
Getting Organized— Informational Writing

This section focuses on the sequential instruction of the Four Square graphic organizer. It begins with activities that are appropriate for your emergent and pre-emergent writers.

Section 2
Other Forms of Composition

Instruction in informational writing is a great place to start because of its logical, organized delivery. However, young writers need experiences in a variety of writing forms. This section provides Four Square teaching tips and examples for the narrative, descriptive, and persuasive styles.

Section 3
Samples of Four Square and Essays

Use these completed organizers and corresponding essays in four different writing styles. These can be models for students, references for instruction, or anchors for your evaluations.

Section 4
Across the Curriculum

Once the Four Square is learned, it is a handy tool for writing across the curriculum. This section provides suggestions for use in history, the sciences, the arts, and even mathematics. If the student is successful in Four Square writing, why not extend that success?

Section 5
Practice Prompts

Topics, topics, topics! Here are a bunch of writing prompts with reproducible pages for student practice.

Section 1
Getting Organized

Brainstorming Ideas

Connecting Ideas

Adding Vivid Language

Elaborating Ideas

Understanding Relationships

We begin our study of organization and prewriting thought process with a focus on the expository style. There are several reasons for teaching this first. One reason is that students typically find this the most daunting type of writing, and mastery of a difficult form builds confidence for future application. However, more importantly, expository writing on a familiar or personal topic is a classic topic of primary grade discourse and journaling. Students want to tell you about the things they know best and all the reasons they love them. These topics are magically convenient for writing and thought organization practice.

The prewriting organization activities used to prepare students for expository writing are identical to those activities required for the descriptive and persuasive forms, so no duplication of effort is needed to transfer skills. However, the instruction will focus on the expository because it allows for a combination of description and persuasion. Suggestions for teaching the difference between styles is included in a later section of this book.

Pre 4□ Activities

Understanding Relationships

In order to organize writing into topics and subtopics, we first need to explore the ways that things are related. Some words, objects or ideas are broad and can encompass other ideas. Beneath these broad words, objects or ideas we can give examples, definitions or subcategories. Before students can develop main idea and supporting detail, they must understand that the subordination of one idea to another is natural and something they have observed in their world.

Provide multiple examples of this relationship's practice. Students can be challenged to think of as many subtopics to an idea as possible, using cereal brands; rock bands; football, baseball, soccer or hockey teams; television programs or any other familiar and comfortable topic. We want students to feel like this is a "game" and to achieve immediate success in writing instruction.

A reproducible worksheet is provided on page 9 for practicing this important concept.

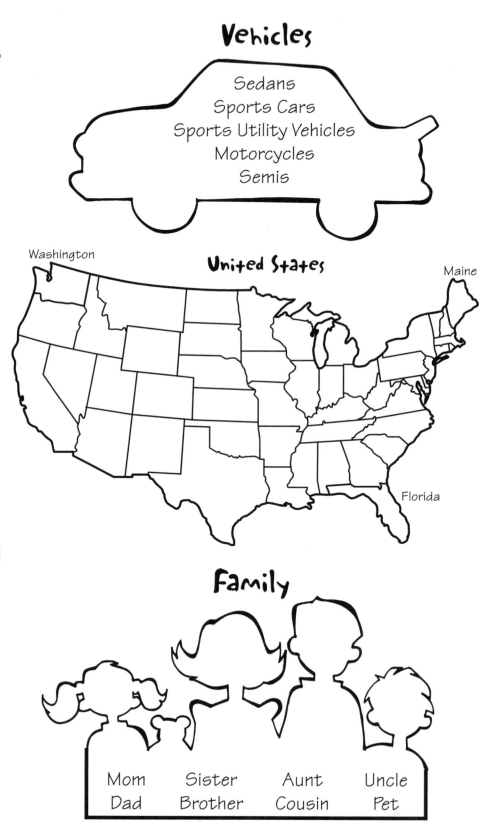

Vehicles

Sedans
Sports Cars
Sports Utility Vehicles
Motorcycles
Semis

United States

Washington   Maine

Florida

Family

Mom   Sister   Aunt   Uncle
Dad   Brother   Cousin   Pet

TLC10581

Understanding Relationships

Directions: Fill in the lines beneath the topic with three items that belong as subtopics.

People

Birds

Things
to Drink

Subjects

_____
_____
_____

_____
_____
_____

_____
_____
_____

_____
_____
_____

4☐

Brainstorming Three Ideas and a Concluding Sentence

In this step, we move our brainstorming into the Four Square format. We will continue our practice in understanding the relationships between ideas. The main, broad, or general idea is placed in the center square of the Four Square (box 1). Boxes 2, 3, and 4 are used for supporting detail.

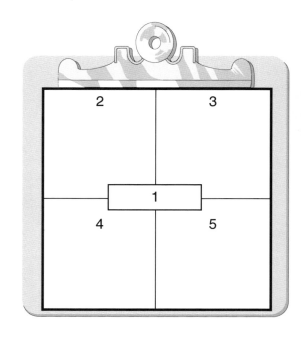

The remaining box, lower right (box 5), will be used to build a summary sentence. In practice this is called the "wrap-up sentence," because it wraps up all the main ideas like a gift with a bow. This contains all the main ideas to focus the future piece of writing. While introducing this sentence so early in instruction (the sentence is a series, requiring commas and conjunctions), the importance of this wrap-up sentence cannot be understated. This sentence will anchor the paper, help writers keep their focus, and provide the seeds to grow both the introductory and concluding sentences. At this point, if students forget commas or conjunctions, don't sweat it. The Four Square is a **prewriting** tool. We can fuss about the conventions when this becomes a draft. Our goal in using the Four Square is to get students thinking!

Eventually we can build this wrap-up sentence into a thesis statement. This will be a sentence containing the main idea and all the major supporting points of the paper. Certainly the thesis isn't a focus of our instruction just yet, but the foundation has been built.

Breaking down the task of writing into a simple, fill-in-the-box brainstorming should make for an engaging challenge for students, even your more reluctant writers!

Practice this very basic Four Square repeatedly. Whole class modeling and cooperative writing are great ways to give your students opportunities to practice. Small groups can brainstorm Four Square ideas on chart paper or overhead transparencies and then share them with the class. The template on the following page can be reproduced to use as an overhead. Mix up the topics by placing a variety of categories in a hat and have the groups randomly draw out topics. Using a cooperative group approach can help to remove intimidation from the writing process and promote the idea that the Four Square is a friendly, game-like approach to writing.

At this stage of instruction on the Four Square, you may remind students that you have only really asked them to write one complete sentence. Of course, you've also asked for a bit more brainstorming and thinking.

The following pages have some reproducible Four Square practice pages.

This example of a basic Four Square shows the relationships between the main idea—"snacks"—and the three supporting details—"pretzels, popcorn, and peanuts."

Pretzels	Popcorn
Peanuts	**Snacks** Pretzels, popcorn and peanuts are snacks.

Name _____

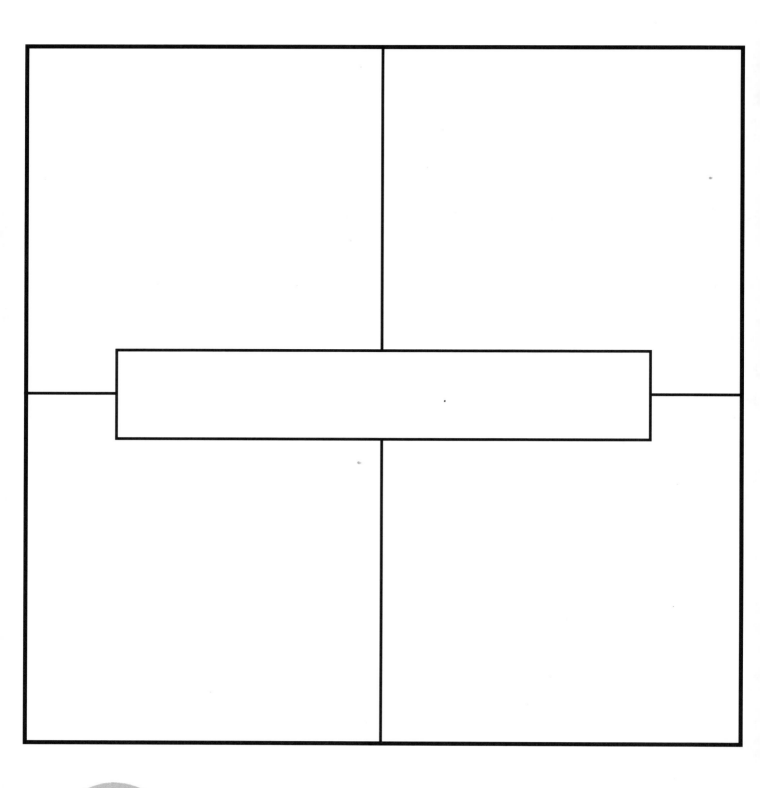

12

TLC10581

Name _____

Directions: Complete the Four Squares with one item in each box and a wrap-up sentence.

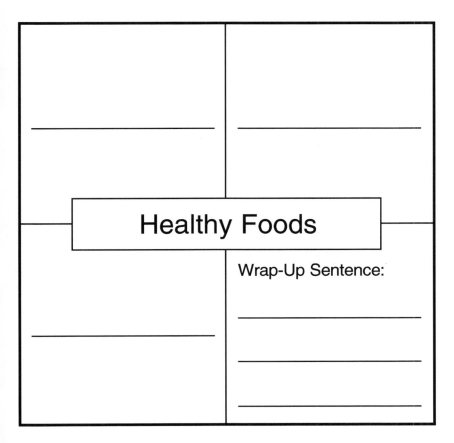

Healthy Foods

Wrap-Up Sentence:

_____

_____

_____

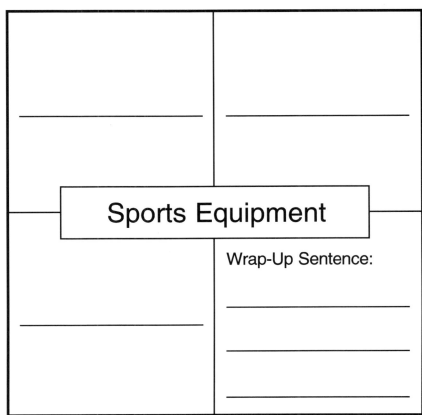

Sports Equipment

Wrap-Up Sentence:

_____

_____

_____

Directions: Complete the Four Squares with one item in each box and a wrap-up sentence.

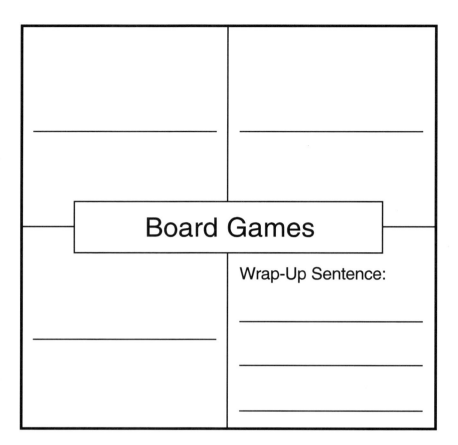

Board Games

Wrap-Up Sentence:

_____

_____

_____

Things in the "Fridge"

Wrap-Up Sentence:

_____

_____

_____

Name _____

Directions: Complete the Four Squares with one item in each box and a wrap-up sentence.

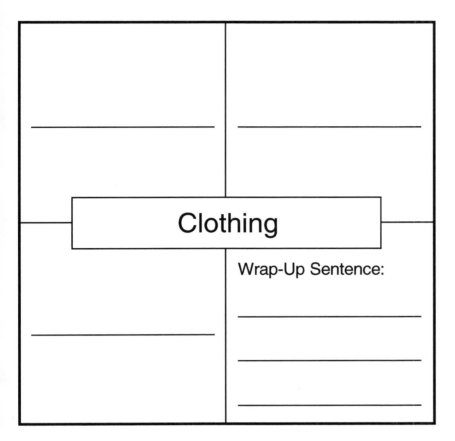

Clothing

Wrap-Up Sentence:

_____

_____

_____

School Subjects

Wrap-Up Sentence:

_____

_____

_____

Directions: Complete the Four Squares with one item in each box and a wrap-up sentence.

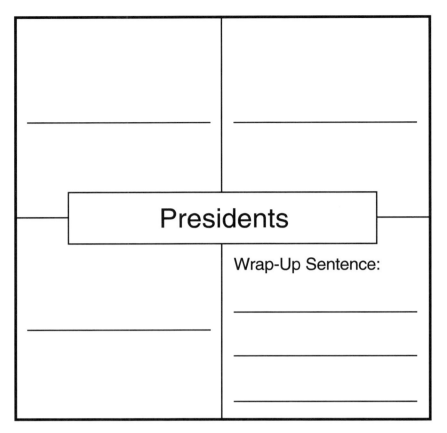

Presidents

Wrap-Up Sentence:

_____

_____

_____

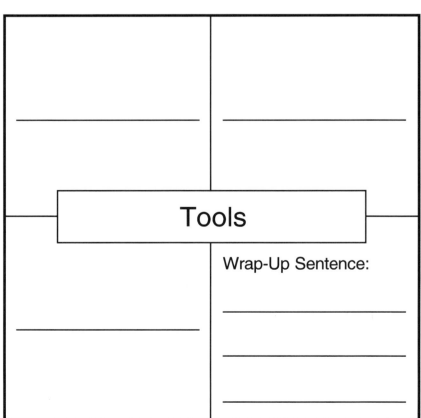

Tools

Wrap-Up Sentence:

_____

_____

_____

TLC10581

Adding a Topic Statement

*Three Supporting Ideas and a Concluding Sentence
Using an Expository or Persuasive-Type Prompt*

Now the stage has been set for developing real logical reasoning and persuasion. The next part of Step 1 involves only a small change in the challenge. The center box will now contain a complete sentence (prompt). In previous exercises there was only a word or short phrase for the topic. The introduction of a complete sentence now alters the requirements of boxes 2, 3 and 4. These boxes must now contain **reasons, examples or explanations** that prove box 1 true. These reasons, examples or explanations must all be different from one another and must be real, quantifiable reasons, not merely matters of opinion.

Students may not easily identify the distinction between fact and opinion. If they believe that "fun," "cool" and "awesome" are quantifiable reasons and different from one another, they will have difficulty building a good persuasive or expository piece of writing. To help them understand that individual perceptions are very different and that an opinion is not reliable, start by telling two stories.

Story 1
> Teacher: I have just heard a great song. It is cool, awesome and great. Do you want to hear it?
>
> Students: (shouting) Yeah!
>
> Teacher: Great. I didn't know you were into opera!

Point out that opera is cool, awesome and great to you, but you may not wish to endure any music that is cool, awesome and great to them.

Story 2
> Teacher: I've got a great new food here. It's delicious, wonderful and so tasty.
>
> Students: (if they fall for it a second time) Yeah!
>
> Teacher: Great. I didn't know you kids liked liver.

For further practice in developing strong supporting details, encourage students to "prove" the topic statement. The ubiquitous courtroom drama on television has exposed kids to a great deal of persuasive argument. This can help to relate the need for quantifiable details. A "Prove It!" reproducible is provided on page 19 for extra practice on this skill.

To provide continuity, it is recommended that you use the same topic as you introduce each new addition to the Four Square. The familiarity and predictability of the topic will facilitate the addition of new layers of detail and complexity in the writing. The "spaghetti and meatballs" example will be used throughout this text, chosen because it is a lunchroom favorite!

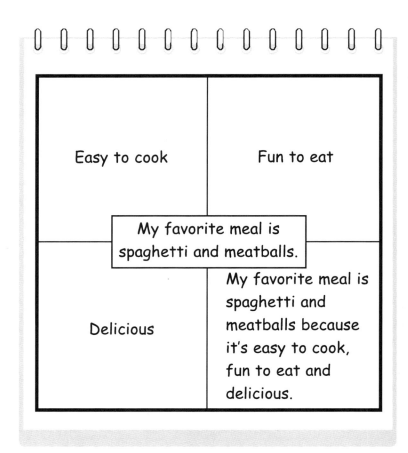

Easy to cook	Fun to eat
My favorite meal is spaghetti and meatballs.	
Delicious	My favorite meal is spaghetti and meatballs because it's easy to cook, fun to eat and delicious.

One area of difficulty that you may encounter at this stage involves the introduction of a conjunction in the wrap-up sentence. *Since*, *because* or *due to* usually work nicely in this situation.

Because the wrap-up is now stringing together different ideas and objects, there is no need to give some attention to the flow of writing in the serial wrap-up sentence.

With modeling and ample group practice (overhead transparency or opaque for sharing), students quickly assimilate the language needed for a nicely flowing wrap-up sentence.

TLC10581

Name _____

Prove It!

Directions: Circle the two reasons that make the best argument for the sentence. Remember to avoid opinions!

1. My school is the best in the world.
   a. It's cool
   b. They pay us to attend
   c. I like it
   d. Candy in the lunchroom

2. The beach makes a good vacation.
   a. Awesome
   b. Super
   c. Cool water
   d. Soft sand

3. Pizza is the best food.
   a. It rules
   b. It's inexpensive
   c. It tastes the best
   d. It has all food groups

4. Basketball is a great sport.
   a. Exciting to watch
   b. Fun to play
   c. Mega, mega cool
   d. It's groovy

5. The best book I ever read was _____

   _____ .

   Give three good reasons. _____

   _____

   _____

   _____

"Prove It" exercise may be completed orally or reproduced to transparency.

Prove It! Answer Key

Directions: Circle the two reasons that make the best argument for the sentence. Remember to avoid opinions!

1. My school is the best in the world.
   a. It's cool
   b. (They pay us to attend)
   c. I like it
   d. (Candy in the lunchroom)

2. The beach makes a good vacation.
   a. Awesome
   b. Super
   c. (Cool water)
   d. (Soft sand)

3. Pizza is the best food.
   a. It rules
   b. (It's inexpensive)
   c. It tastes the best
   d. (It has all food groups)

4. Basketball is a great sport.
   a. (Exciting to watch)
   b. (Fun to play)
   c. Mega, mega cool
   d. It's groovy

TLC10581

Name _____

Directions: Write a reason, example or explanation in each box to support the main idea sentence in the center box and write a wrap-up sentence.

_____   _____

It is important to have friends.

_____

_____

_____

_____

_____

_____

TLC10581

Directions: Write a reason, example or explanation in each box to support the main idea sentence in the center box and write a wrap-up sentence.

My family is
very special.

TLC10581

Name _____

_____

_____

Bicycle helmets are important.

_____

_____

_____

_____

_____

Step 2

4☐ + 3

Adding Supporting Details

Now we are ready to consider the further development of the details in boxes 2, 3, and 4. In a sense, these boxes will now be "Four Squared" independently. These details will be developed later to make up the meat of the paragraphs in the body of the composition. Using Four Square ensures that the details are aligned with main ideas, and that a topic sentence focuses each body paragraph.

Students may not be so easily convinced of this need for expansion of their thoughts. One way to point out the need for elaboration is to "read" the story created by Four Square alone.

It's easy	It's fun to eat
My favorite meal is spaghetti and meatballs.	
It's delicious	My favorite meal is spaghetti and meatballs because it's easy, fun to eat and delicious.

Adding detail and support poses difficulty for some students. Many are not accustomed to elaborating. Writing is not like a multiple-choice examination, and starting their brains may be painful for some kids!

The story created by our example would read as follows:

> My favorite meal is spaghetti and meatballs. My favorite meal is spaghetti and meatballs because it's easy. My favorite meal is spaghetti and meatballs because it's fun to eat. My favorite meal is spaghetti and meatballs because it's delicious. My favorite meal is spaghetti and meatballs because it's easy, fun to eat and delicious.

If read orally, the students will identify the repetition and need for detail to enhance the story.

TLC10581

Occasionally students will need some prompting to expand on their subject. For an item in boxes 2, 3, and 4, ask students to prove, clarify, or give examples of the subject at the top of the box. Questions such as, "What's so good about it?" or "What's great about this reason/example?" often engage the students' imaginations a bit.

It is important to remind students that *there should not be a repetition* anywhere on the Four Square.

It's easy
- roll up meat
- throw in pot
- pour store-bought sauce

It's fun to eat
- twirl on fork
- slurp it
- splatter the sauce

My favorite meal is spaghetti and meatballs.

It's delicious
- tomatoes
- Italian spices
- filling meat

My favorite meal is spaghetti and meatballs because it's easy to make, fun to eat and delicious.

Although you have not yet asked students to take their writing off the organizer and into paragraph form, it is valuable to read them the essay in its formation. At this stage this is the essay.

Because of the difficulty that some students experience during this step of instruction, it is recommended that there be ample opportunity to practice. The lessons work well in a modeling, as group work, and as individual drills. Using chart paper or an overhead, have students work in groups with a *recorder* doing the writing and a *reporter* to read the Four Square aloud to the rest of the class.

At this stage, you can reveal to the students that they have already done much of the work of writing a five-paragraph essay!

My favorite meal is spaghetti and meatballs.

My favorite meal is spaghetti and meatballs because it's easy. You simply roll up the meat, then throw it in the pot, and pour on the store-bought sauce.

My favorite meal is spaghetti and meatballs because it's fun to eat. I like to twirl it on my fork. It is fun to slurp. I always splatter the sauce.

My favorite meal is spaghetti and meatballs because it's delicious. I like the taste of tomatoes. The Italian spices are great. The meat is very filling.

My favorite meal is spaghetti and meatballs because it's easy, fun to eat and delicious.

 Additional activities on adding supporting details can be found on the enhanced CD.

Name _____

Directions: Write a reason, example or explanation in each box to support the main idea sentence in the center box. Then give three details for each and write a wrap-up sentence.

_____

- _____

- _____

- _____

_____

- _____

- _____

- _____

I would like to visit _____ .

_____

- _____

- _____

- _____

_____

_____

_____

Directions: *Write a reason, example or explanation in each box to support the main idea sentence in the center box. Then give three details for each and write a wrap-up sentence.*

_____

- _____

- _____

- _____

_____

- _____

- _____

- _____

My college major might be _____ .

_____

- _____

- _____

- _____

_____

_____

_____

Evaluating Our Progress

a Checklist for Consideration

When the students have achieved a general competency in the Four Square Plus Three, it is appropriate to do a Four Square evaluation. To determine progress in the use of the Four Square, give students a one-sentence prompt for the center box. About fifteen minutes of time should be adequate for completion of the Four Square. Even when using a detailed organizer like the Four Square, we need to remind students that the bulk of our time and effort in writing is for the drafting. Four Square, a *prewriting* tool, can help us with our drafting, but it shouldn't take all day!

Below is a checklist that is a useful instrument in evaluating Four Square Plus Three.

Evaluating 4□ + 3

Student Name: _____

		Yes	No
1.	Are the Four Square reasons quantifiable and not opinions?	____	____
2.	Is there repetition of detail?	____	____
3.	Are the details logical expansion of the reasons?	____	____
4.	Are the details quantifiable or factual and free of opinion?	____	____
5.	Are there gross mechanical problems in the wrap-up sentence?	____	____

TLC10581

Step 3

4□ + 3 + C

Adding Connecting Words to Provide Transition Between Thoughts

By now students are developing their thesis (box 1) into three reasons, examples or explanations (boxes 2, 3 and 4) and supporting elaboration. Because the three reasons, examples or explanations are different from one another, the essay is in need of a connection of these differing ideas to provide flow and readability.

Transition words, or as the formula calls them, CONNECTING words, can bridge the gap between ideas. If there are two similar ideas, there is an appropriate connecting word to link them. If there are contrasting ideas, there are words that key us to the difference. These connecting words also provide smooth reading when changing paragraphs. Use of these words is critical to successful writing. In fact, it is so critical that students should not be asked to remember them. Color-code connecting words on wall posters, and make them available whenever students write. (See pages 32-34.)

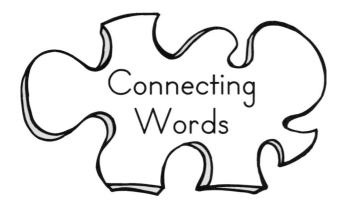

To introduce the concept of connecting words to students, ask for a show of hands of those who have ever worked a puzzle. Most students can identify a puzzle piece and are familiar with its design. Explain that connecting words are the "little sticking out part" of the puzzle piece; they are words that do the same job as that part. Connecting words hold the different pieces of an essay together.

This explanation lends itself well to the presentation of the connecting word wall posters. To ensure success, the words are color coded. Because box 1 is the beginning of the piece, no connection is necessary. Box 2 is coded green (*green* means "go"). Boxes 3 and 4 are yellow to signify moving along cautiously. Box 5 is red, for we are preparing to stop.

Students love choosing connecting words. They absolutely cannot get this stage "wrong" as long as they select the word from the appropriate list. This fosters confidence in students, and this "easy" stage is a break from the more intense brain work required in "+3."

Again provide ample practice with this new step of instruction in modeling, group and individual settings.

The following pages are wall posters and workbook pages for this step.

First	Also
It's easy • roll up meat • throw in pot • pour store-bought sauce	It's fun to eat • twirl on fork • slurp it • splatter the sauce

My favorite meal is spaghetti and meatballs.

Third	So you can see
It's delicious • tomatoes • Italian spices • filling meat	My favorite meal is spaghetti and meatballs because it's easy to make, fun to eat and delicious.

Continue to read aloud all examples as they are completed. This will facilitate the change over to composition.

The oral reading of our essay at this stage (Remember, students are writing *only in Four Square form*.):

My favorite meal is spaghetti and meatballs.

First, my favorite meal is spaghetti and meatballs because it's easy. You simply roll up the meat, then throw it in the pot and pour on the store-bought sauce.

Also, my favorite meal is spaghetti and meatballs because it's fun to eat. I like to twirl it on my fork. It's fun to slurp. I always splatter the sauce.

Third, my favorite meal is spaghetti and meatballs because it's delicious. I like the taste of tomatoes. The Italian spices are great. The meat is very filling.

So you can see, my favorite meal is spaghetti and meatballs because it's easy, fun to eat and delicious.

30

Wall Poster

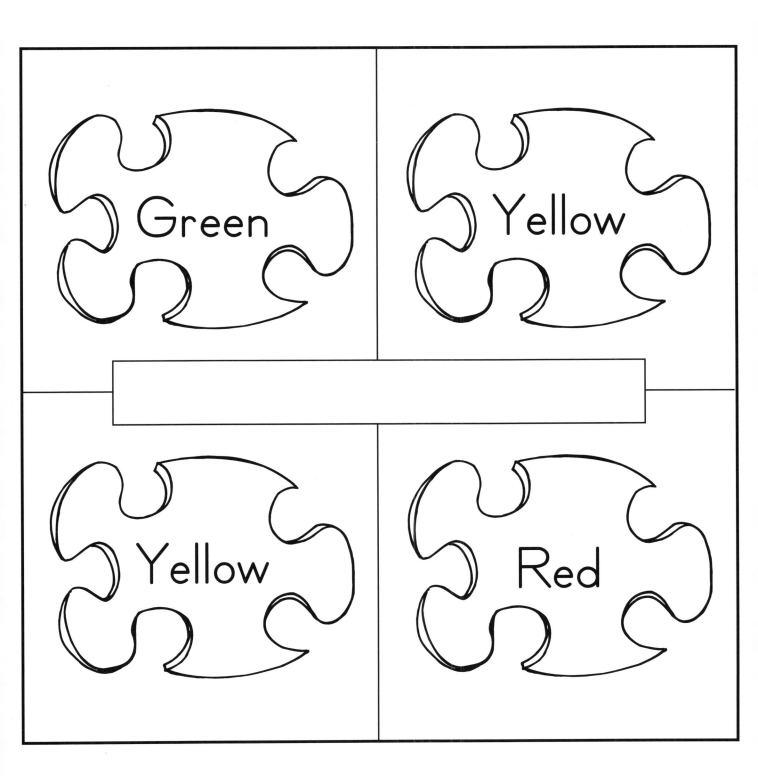

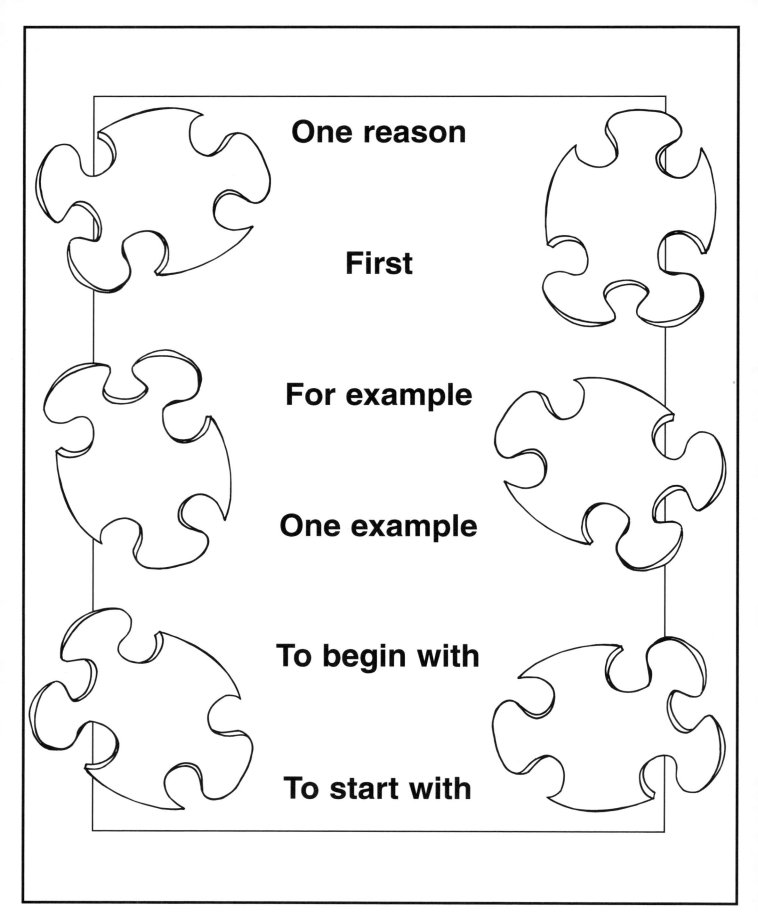

One reason

First

For example

One example

To begin with

To start with

Color the border of this poster green.

TLC10581

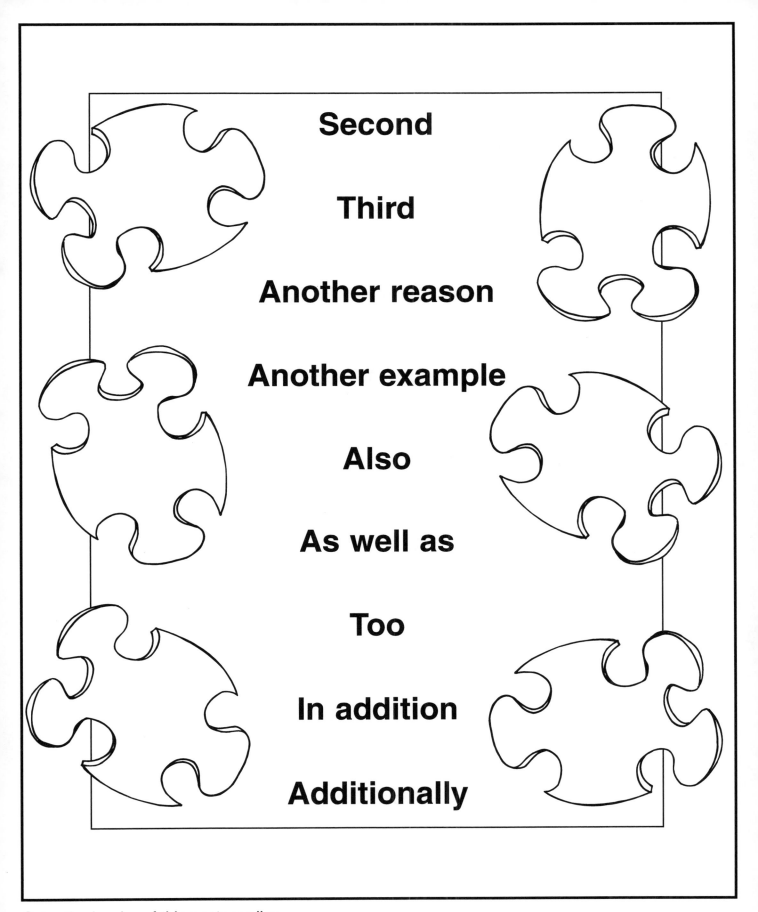

Second

Third

Another reason

Another example

Also

As well as

Too

In addition

Additionally

Color the border of this poster yellow.

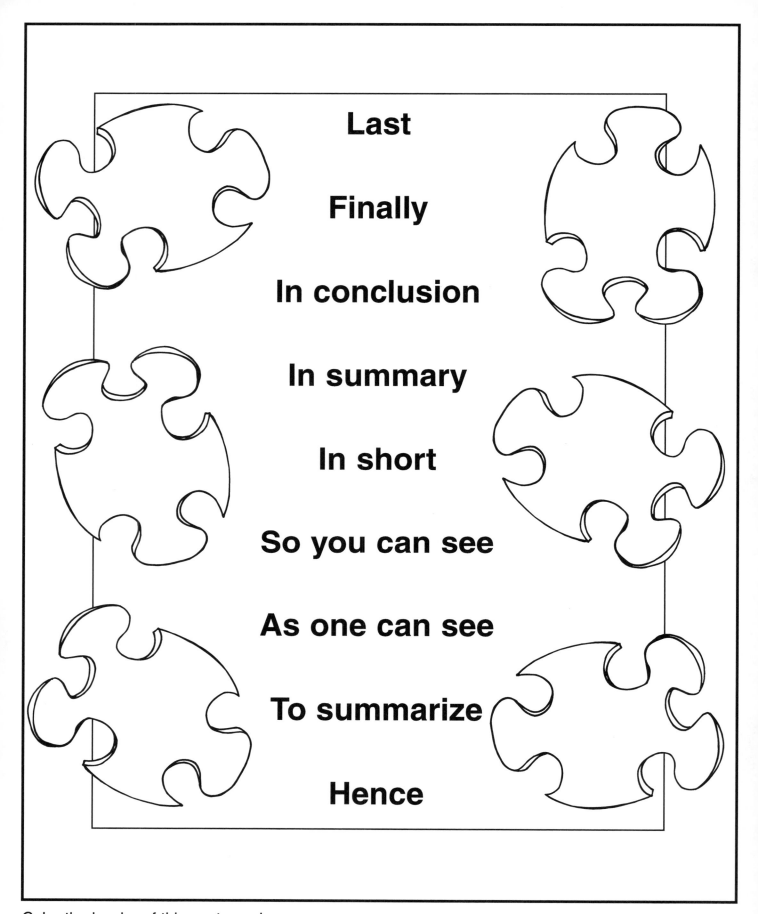

Last

Finally

In conclusion

In summary

In short

So you can see

As one can see

To summarize

Hence

Color the border of this poster red.

TLC10581

Directions: Write a reason, example or explanation in each box to support the main idea sentence in the center box. Give three details for each. Then choose connecting words.

Puzzle Piece

- _____

- _____

- _____

Puzzle Piece

- _____

- _____

- _____

Everyone should participate in a sport.

Puzzle Piece

- _____

- _____

- _____

Puzzle Piece

_____

_____

_____

TLC10581

35

Name _____

Directions: Write a reason, example or explanation in each box to support the main idea sentence in the center box. Give three details for each. Then choose connecting words.

Puzzle Piece

- _____

- _____

- _____

Puzzle Piece

- _____

- _____

- _____

Just say no to drugs.

Puzzle Piece

- _____

- _____

- _____

Puzzle Piece

_____

_____

_____

TLC10581

Step 4

4□ + 3 + C + V

Incorporating Vivid Language into Writing

Thus far instruction on the Four Square organizer has had the goal of building focus, organization and supporting detail into students' writing. This fourth step of instruction begins to assist the writer in developing a style and to use writing as a craft.

Writing with vivid language is achieved by careful, specific word choice. Sensory experiences are an excellent means of providing a vivid expression of thought. Vivid language in writing lets us know what the writer sees, hears, feels, smells and tastes. Vivid language is also heavily involved with the emotional state of the writer. Sometimes vivid language gives an example that provides a more specific image for the reader.

To explain the need for vivid language, students can be drawn to a favorite medium–television. If you want to explain everything that happened on a particular program that night, you can say there was a "really cool car chase" on a favorite detective show. Or you can say, "There was a detective show where this guy was chasing a '97 red Camaro at high speed up and down the hills of San Francisco. They went squealing past rows of tall, brown apartment buildings. The police car screeched around a corner and whacked into a mailbox. Then the police slammed into a trolley car and, boom, it went up into flames. Meanwhile the bad guys zipped across the Golden Gate until they lost control of their Camaro. The tires were screaming. Then they went silently over the edge until their demise in a tiny splash in the gleaming blue waters below." Ask students in which interpretation is the more vivid description? In which can you picture the action?

To encourage the use of vivid language, students need to be probed. When applying a vivid word to a particular detail, you need to ask students some questions. For instance, if your detail states "a pepperoni pizza," ask students: How does the pizza look? How does it taste? What do you hear? How does it feel? How does it smell? What are your emotions at the particular moment you encounter the pizza? The answers to these questions clarify the composition for the potential reader by giving us more of the picture that the writer "sees" in the mind's eye.

Vivid language writing is not developed overnight, but there are certain techniques that can be employed to encourage its growth. Students can build "Like What?" lists. For instance, a certain attribute may be overused and not provide a vivid enough picture for the reader. The "Like What?" list can be used to give alternate word choices for the writer. It is also an easy way to get students to include a literary device–simile or metaphor.

The "Like What?" exercise can be used to produce some ready references to help writers avoid using jaded language to describe objects or events. Students can generate lists from brainstorming or thesaurus use and post them in a word wall reference area for writers.

*You may need to remind students to not get **carried away** with this. They could develop "like" fever!*

Cold	Good	Blue
ice	as gold	the ocean
Alaska	whipped cream on hot cocoa	the sky
Grandma's hands	air conditioning in the summer	an angel's eyes
a soda can		a blueberry

TLC10581

A "Like What?" reproducible is on page 41 so that you can start producing those lists.

On page 40 is a vivid words poster which reminds student writers to engage their five-senses-plus-one when providing vivid language.

Addition of vivids enhances the maturity of writing. This further level of elaboration, usually on a sensory level, helps the writer develop voice. Building these descriptions prepares the young writer for longer compositions.

Continue to read aloud all examples as they are completed. This will facilitate the change over to composition.

First
    It's easy
- roll up meat
  golf balls
- throw in pot
  huge cauldron-size
- pour store-bought sauce
  Mama someone or other

Also
    It's fun to eat
- twirl on fork
  looks like a twister
- slurp it
  loud smacking noise
- splatter the sauce
  like an explosion

My favorite meal is spaghetti and meatballs.

Third
    It's delicious
- tomatoes
  red and tangy
- Italian spices
  zippy garlic
- filling meat
  like a hamburger

So you can see
My favorite meal is spaghetti and meatballs because it's easy to make, fun to eat and delicious.

The oral reading of our essay at this stage (Remember, students are writing *only in Four Square form* this far.):

My favorite meal is spaghetti and meatballs.

First, my favorite meal is spaghetti and meatballs because it's easy. You simply roll up the meat into golf ball-sized pieces, then throw it in the pot. I use a huge, cauldron-size pot. Pour on the store-bought sauce. My favorite brand is Mama someone or other.

Also, my favorite meal is spaghetti and meatballs because it's fun to eat. I like to twirl it on my fork. It looks just like a twister. It's fun to slurp because it makes a loud smacking noise. I always splatter the sauce. When I'm done, it looks like an explosion.

Third, my favorite meal is spaghetti and meatballs because it's delicious. I like the tangy taste of red tomatoes. The Italian spices are great, especially the zippy garlic. The meat is very filling, like a hamburger.

So you can see, my favorite meal is spaghetti and meatballs because it's easy, fun to eat and delicious.

Pages 40-43 are wall posters and workbook pages for this step.

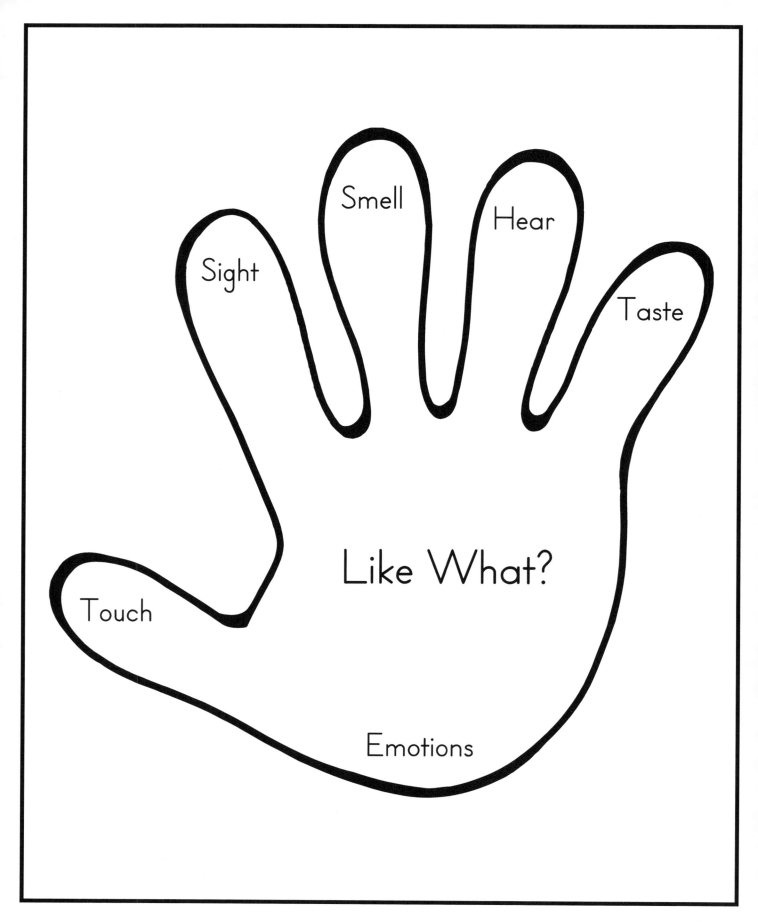

Vivid Words Poster

Like What?

Name _____

Directions: Write a reason, example or explanation in each box to support the main idea sentence in the center box. Give three details for each. Then choose connecting words. Supply one vivid for each detail and circle it.

Puzzle Piece

- _____

- _____

- _____

Puzzle Piece

- _____

- _____

- _____

Teens should have more freedom.

Puzzle Piece

- _____

- _____

- _____

Puzzle Piece

_____

_____

_____

42

Name _____

Directions: Write a reason, example or explanation in each box to support the main idea sentence in the center box. Give three details for each. Then choose connecting words. Supply one vivid for each detail and circle it.

Puzzle Piece

- _____

- _____

- _____

Puzzle Piece

- _____

- _____

- _____

My favorite season is _____ .

Puzzle Piece

- _____

- _____

- _____

Puzzle Piece

_____

_____

_____

Evaluating Our Progress
A Checklist for Consideration

Evaluating student work during instruction in the Four Square may prevent the need to do the dreaded rewrite once the draft is completed. In evaluating the Four Square + 3 + C + V, look for a variety and richness of detail. Also, there should be additional information added through the use of vivids.

Evaluating 4☐ + 3 + C + V

Student Name: _____

		Yes	No
1.	Are the Four Square reasons quantifiable and not opinion?	____	____
2.	Is there repetition of detail?	____	____
3.	Are the details logical expansion of the reasons?	____	____
4.	Are the details quantifiable or factual and free of opinion?	____	____
5.	Are there gross mechanical problems in the wrap-up sentence?	____	____
6.	Is there value added information from the vivids?	____	____

TLC10581

4☐ + 3 + C + V + E

Making It Personal—Adding Elaboration

Elaboration
(the Big E)

E
xample
xperience
vidence

Instruction on the Four Square thus far has focused primarily on the organization of the information. We have practiced placing details into the appropriate boxes, and we've added transitional devices and vivid language. Now we need to make the writing more specific and personal with the addition of *elaboration*, sometimes called the "Big E" of writing.

First It's easy	Also It's fun to eat

• roll up meat
  golf balls
• throw in pot
  huge cauldron-size
• pour store-bought
  sauce
  Mama someone or other
	• twirl on fork
	  looks like a twister
	• slurp it
	  loud smacking noise
	• splatter the sauce
	  like an explosion

My favorite meal is spaghetti and meatballs.

Third It's delicious	So you can see

• tomatoes
  red and tangy
• Italian spices
  zippy garlic
• filling meat
  like a hamburger
	My favorite meal is spaghetti and meat-balls because it's easy to make, fun to eat and delicious.

Elaborating means making it very specific. We can elaborate the #2 box of the "spaghetti" Four Square by adding a personal **experience**. The "it's easy" idea can be proven by describing this experience.

> "I remember one time my cousins called and said that they were on their way for a surprise visit. They were only hour away, but my mom had dinner ready in time for everyone. Spaghetti dinner for 12 was hot and delicious!"

This experience proves that making spaghetti and meatball is easy. In the Four Square, a planning tool, we need not write the whole experience. The key words "cousin visit" in a circle in that box are all the writer needs as a reminder to elaborate that box.

For box #3, the circled phrase "baby bib" would translate to **evidence**.

> "If you need evidence that this meal is messy, you need only look at my baby sister Deb's bib when we have spaghetti. It's covered with sauce, cheese and meat!"

Box #4 may use an **example** with the phrase "School Spaghetti."

> "On spaghetti day in school, my friends and I always bring extra coins from home to get doubles. It tastes so good we can all slurp down a double helping of this awesome dish at lunch."

The elaborated experience, example, or evidence helps students to make the writing more specific and personal, and helps to bring a bit more character to the writing. While we all may cite the ease, taste, and mess of spaghetti, we can draw on the personal to elaborate. The circled key words often grow into 2-3 sentences in the body paragraphs, increasing the specificity of the writing.

Try using some of the Four Square prompts from the previous pages and ask students to add their experiences, evidence, and examples (Big E Elaboration).

Additional information on encouraging extended elaboration can be found on the enhanced CD.

Rote Instruction
4☐ + 3 + C + V = 5 Paragraphs
Taking the Writing off the Organizer

Students have now spent a great deal of time working on the organizer, having never completed the composition phase of the writing process. The oral "story readings" performed with the completed Four Squares at early stages should have led to the understanding that this was a part of a bigger scheme.

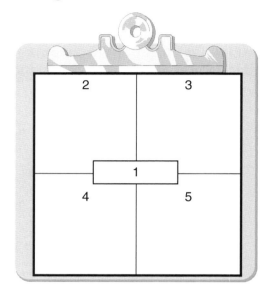

When introducing the concept of moving the information from the Four Square to the multiple-paragraph essay, it is generally recommended to do a rote lesson. The whole class or group can build a Four Square together. Then the story is built one sentence at a time. Use chart paper or an overhead transparency with a simulated piece of notebook paper.

As the composition is being modeled one sentence at a time, students copy it. This "down time" can be used for instant remediation and reminders of the rules of writing in paragraphs. The beauty of the Four Square is that each time a new box is encountered, it is time to indent. The difficulty of paragraphing has been handled during prewriting.

The Four Square has built in a good self-checking mechanism for sentence building. Since each of boxes 2, 3 and 4 had four items in them, students can be reminded to check for four capital letters and four periods in each of the corresponding paragraphs.

Remind students never to take the shortcut of trying to list all items in each box as one long sentence. Not only is this poor writing practice, but it is bound to be a run-on sentence.

On pages 47-50 are exercises where the Four Square is given, and students need only make the transfer of skill to composition.

Additional examples of completed Four Squares and resulting essays can be found on the enhanced CD.

TLC10581

Name _____

Directions: For the given Four Square, write the information in the five-paragraph format.

```
┌─────────────────────────────┬─────────────────────────────┐
│ One reason                  │ Also                        │
│       Sleep In              │       Play Around           │
│  • wear pajamas             │  • roller blade             │
│    flannel                  │    around neighborhood      │
│  • don't shower             │  • board games              │
│    until afternoon          │    Monopoly™                │
│  • lounge around            │  • cards                    │
│    no rushing               │    Gin Rummy                │
│  (Saturday cartoons in PJs) │ (3-day Monopoly game over   │
│                             │  Memorial Day weekend)      │
├──────────┐ Weekends are great. ┌──────────┤
│ As well as              │ In conclusion               │
│    Stay Up Late         │                             │
│  • sleepovers           │ Weekends are great          │
│    pillow fights        │ because you can             │
│  • scary movies         │ sleep in, play around       │
│    big monsters         │ and stay up late.           │
│  • popcorn              │                             │
│    buttery              │                             │
│ (My two best friends slept over │                       │
│  for a monster movie marathon)  │                       │
└─────────────────────────────┴─────────────────────────────┘
```

Paragraph 1

_____

_____

_____

_____

_____

Paragraph 2

_____

_____

_____

_____

_____

Paragraph 3

_____

_____

_____

_____

_____

Paragraph 4

_____

_____

_____

_____

_____

Paragraph 5

_____

_____

_____

_____

_____

Did you indent each paragraph (five times)?
Do you have your capitals and periods?
Did you write from margin to margin?

TLC10581

Directions: *For the given Four Square, write the information in the five-paragraph format.*

First	Second
Honesty	**Pay Taxes**

• truthful
  always
• no cheating
  on tests
• confessing
  mistakes
	• on time
	  before April 15
	• with pride
	  patriotism
	• every year
	  for rest of life

(Mom's broken lamp)	(post office and dinner ritual)

A good citizen has many traits.

Too	Hence
Follow Laws	

• traffic laws
  speed limits
• never steal
  robbery
• never fight
  assault
	A good citizen has many traits such as honesty, paying taxes and following laws.

(farm stand with unmanned cash box)	

Paragraph 1

_____

_____

_____

_____

_____

_____

Paragraph 2

_____

_____

_____

_____

Paragraph 3

_____

_____

_____

_____

Paragraph 4

_____

_____

_____

_____

Paragraph 5

_____

_____

_____

_____

Did you indent each paragraph (five times)?
Do you have your capitals and periods?
Did you write from margin to margin?

TLC10581

Improving the Introduction Paragraph

Writing That Thesis Statement

The introductory paragraph is perhaps the most important paragraph in a composition. It is the first impression made on the reader. Also, the first paragraph makes a promise. Explain to the students that the first paragraph in a composition sets the tone of the composition in much the same way that a topic sentence sets the theme of the paragraph. The first paragraph will be used to promise the topic of discourse, as well as prepare the reader for the details to come.

The beauty of the Four Square writing method is that nearly all the troubles faced in composition will be addressed in the organization stage of the writing process. Students at the secondary level are often asked to write a thesis statement and paper. In the Four Square, the students have already prepared this information. By writing the wrap-up sentence in box 5 very early in the learning of the Four Square, students have already practiced this skill.

The first paragraph can now be expanded beyond the one topic sentence. Before the topic sentence, we will add an eye-catcher, hook, or lead. The topic sentence will follow. Then the writer can use the three ideas from the tops of boxes 2, 3, and 4 to preview the main points of the paper. For the final sentence of the introduction, the writer can use a personal feeling, reflection, or a thought-provoking statement to bridge into the body of the composition. Now the reader knows the topic, the main points that will be developed, and the writer's connection or reflection on the topic!

First Paragraph

1. Hook/Lead

2. Topic sentence

3. Preview of main ideas

4. Connection/reflection

A Very Short List of Leads

The Question

Where can you find great nutrition and fun? In a bowl of spaghetti and meatballs!

The Quotation

"Mamma mia! It's so delicious!"

Hyperbole

I could eat a whole sea of spaghetti, or a mountain of meatballs.

Fragments (Chains)

Meatballs. Spices. Hearty slurping noises. These are just a few of the things I like about spaghetti and meatballs.

Famous Name or Place

Chef Boyardee wouldn't stand a chance against my mom's spaghetti and meatballs.

Money

Ten million dollars, or a really good bowl of spaghetti and meatballs? The choice is clear for me.

Statistics

Four essential minerals and seven vitamins are among the many benefits of spaghetti and meatballs.

Onomatopoeia

Slurp! Smack! Gulp! Mmmmm! That's the sound of good eating and spaghetti and meatballs.

Add your own:

_____

_____

_____

_____

TLC10581

Directions: Write the first paragraph for each Four Square. Be sure to write topic, wrap-up and personal sentences.

It is important to get a good education.

It is important to get a good education so you can get a job, be successful and feel good about yourself.

_____

_____

_____

_____

_____

_____

Name _____

Directions: Write the first paragraph for each Four Square. Be sure to write topic, wrap-up and personal sentences.

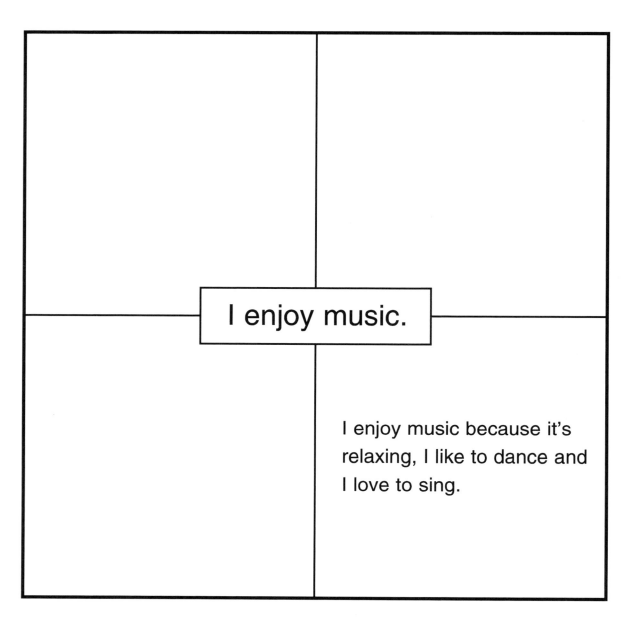

I enjoy music.

I enjoy music because it's relaxing, I like to dance and I love to sing.

_____
_____
_____
_____
_____
_____

TLC10581

Improving the Final Paragraph

Concluding the Composition

The concluding paragraph in composition carries a great deal of weight. In expository or persuasive writing, this is the writer's final chance to bring home the message to the reader. It is to be used for summary and final emphasis of the main idea.

Using the wrap-up sentence in combination with a "red" connecting word works well in bringing closure to the composition. The recounting of ideas should bring the reader full circle, and the connecting word signifies that this is the composition's end.

At this point of the composition we do not want to add any new information, because it would not be developed. However, after the final wrap-up sentence, it may be appropriate to add a reflective or personal sentence. Encouraging students to end with an exclamatory or interrogative sentence usually gets them thinking. It is also an easy way to get them to add variety to sentence structure.

Final Paragraph

1. Wrap-Up Sentence with Connecting Word

2. Personal/Reflective Sentence, Question, Exclamation, or Ending Zinger

This formula is an easy way to conclude the composition. Encourage students to make that personal sentence perky!

A Very Short List of Ending Zingers

Advice
If you want to have a healthy life, you need eat well. Spaghetti and meatballs is a good start.

Big Feeling
Spaghetti and meatballs reminds me of home, healthy eating, and happiness.

Remember
Remember, spaghetti and meatballs is a good choice for food and fun.

Do
Get yourself some spaghetti and meatballs right away.

Future
Maybe, in the future, we will see this delicious meal on our school lunch menu. It's sure to be a hit!

Lesson
I have learned that spaghetti and meatballs can be just as healthy as it is tasty. A great meal all around!

Recommendation
My recommendation? Get some spaghetti and meatballs today!

Main idea, simply
Spaghetti and meatballs. Good food and good fun.

Question
Wouldn't you like some right now?

Your thoughts
Thinking of all the tasty flavors and the great fun, my mouth is watering for some spaghetti and meatballs.

Wish, Hope, Dream
I hope we're having some tonight.

Dedication
Mmm, I love the taste and feel of spaghetti and meatballs. Thank you, cafeteria ladies, for making such a wonderful lunch!

TLC10581

Directions: *Write the final paragraph for each Four Square. Be sure to include the wrap-up and a personal sentence, question, exclamation, or ending zinger.*

My favorite dessert is pie a la mode.

My favorite dessert is pie a la mode because I like the crust, filling, and ice cream.

_____

_____

_____

_____

_____

Directions: Write the final paragraph for each Four Square. Be sure to include the wrap-up and a personal sentence, question, exclamation, or ending zinger.

It is important to have a goal.	
	It is important to have a goal because it keeps you focused, gives you hope and makes you stronger.

_____
_____
_____
_____
_____

Section 2
Other Forms of Composition

Informational

Narrative

Persuasive

Descriptive

The Narrative Style

Using the Four Square to Plan a Creative Story

Narrative writing is quite different from the informational writing types we've examined so far. A narrative is largely dependent on creativity. To craft a narrative, the writer must be able to devise a setting, characters, or situation from his or her imagination. Informational writing required the writers to employ imagination, but the basic foundation of the writing was to deliver some concrete information.

While stories and narratives do grow from the imagination, there are structural foundations to be taught. A story will usually have a central focus, or main idea. This is different from the thesis type of main idea that drives informational writing. Too often beginning writers miss the main idea and then create stories lacking focus.

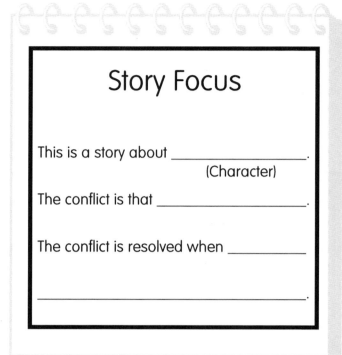

Story Focus

This is a story about _____.
                                         (Character)

The conflict is that _____.

The conflict is resolved when _____

_____.

Have you witnessed student narrative story writing that meanders, often changing setting or action without explanation? Probably what these stories are missing is a central conflict. Before using the Four Square for story planning, it is important to help students to understand the *story focus*.

Practice the story focus using familiar stories. For example:

> This is a story about the big, bad wolf.
>
> The conflict is that he wants three "pork chops" for supper.
>
> The conflict is resolved when the pigs outwit him in a house of bricks.
>
> Or
>
> This is a story about a precocious girl with golden hair.
>
> The conflict is that she chooses to trespass into a house of bears.
>
> The conflict is resolved when the bears scare her out of a stolen sleep.

60

Practice this story focus using picture books. Yes, picture books are likely below the reading level of most of your students, but one of the great things about picture books is their accessibility. Using multiple shorter, simpler texts, students can practice story focus and story mapping on a Four Square.

Explain to students that there are major differences between the narrative and informational styles, as highlighted in this chart.

Informational

- Main goal – to inform
- Uses reasons, examples
- Visibly structured
- Thesis and development

Narrative

- Main goal – to entertain
- Uses events, emotions
- Structured by change over time
- Characters and actions

Another way to illustrate the difference is to compare and contrast two Four Squares on a similar prompt, one with a narrative interpretation and one with an informational interpretation.

Topic: The best day of my life

Informational

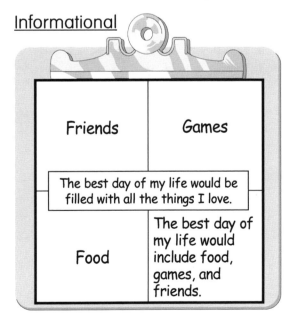

Friends	Games
The best day of my life would be filled with all the things I love.	
Food	The best day of my life would include food, games, and friends.

Narrative

Jumped from plane	Landed safely
I received a birthday gift from my friends.	
Meet the president	Celebrated with my favorite—chocolate cake

The narrative Four Square shows the ACTION!

Additional examples of informational and narrative Four Squares and resulting essays can be found on the enhanced CD.

4☐

narrative Writing

The Four Square is a tool to help writers organize the structure of their writing. In narrative writing, we can teach story structure based on the elements of a story:

Characters & Setting
Conflict
Rise in Action
Climax
Resolution/Denouement

Again, using picture books to practice the story elements will help the beginning writers to identify and then build these elements in their own stories. We can use the boxes of the Four Square to map our ideas for these elements.

The 4☐ stage in a narrative style

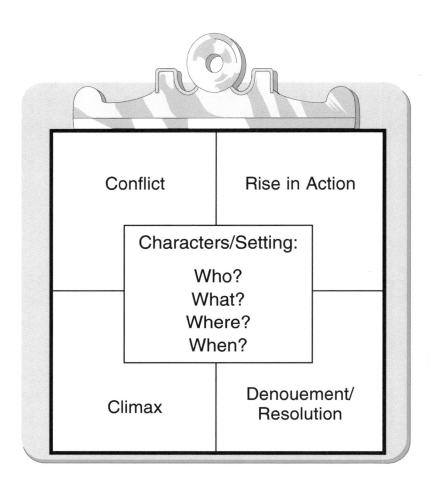

Conflict	Rise in Action
Characters/Setting: Who? What? Where? When?	
Climax	Denouement/ Resolution

To help students develop the characters and setting (box #1), answer the four "W" questions about the scene before the conflict happened. Who was there, where they were, when was it, and what were they doing before things got interesting?

After the setting is established, the narrative Four Square can be completed with STRONG ACTION words for the conflict, rise in action, climax and denouement/resolution of the story.

TLC10581

Name _____

Directions: Complete the setting, events and ending for the narrative style Four Square.

A time I disobeyed

Conflict	Rise in Action
_____	_____
_____	_____
_____	_____
_____	_____

Who? _____

What? _____

Where? _____

When? _____

Climax	Denouement/ Resolution
_____	_____
_____	_____
_____	_____
_____	_____

Directions: Complete the setting, events and ending for the narrative style Four Square.

My sibling read my diary.

Conflict	Rise in Action
_____	_____
_____	_____
_____	_____
_____	_____

Who? _____

What? _____

Where? _____

When? _____

Climax	Denouement/ Resolution
_____	_____
_____	_____
_____	_____
_____	_____

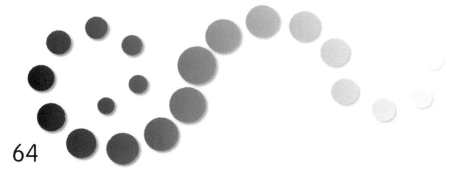

TLC10581

4□ + 3

narrative

The "+3" step in building a narrative Four Square is somewhat different from the informational form. In the narrative form, we will use the details to keep the story moving forward, providing more information for the reader. With the details, we can help the reader to fully envision the story, including sensory detail, characters' emotions, and vivid description.

To further this goal, it is helpful to ask students to focus on developing each part of the story by adding details about what the characters can see, hear, and how they may feel. If the story calls for additional senses, students can also add the senses of touch, smell and taste. Get your students started with this by placing the eye (see), ear (hear) and heart (feelings) icons in each box for brainstorming.

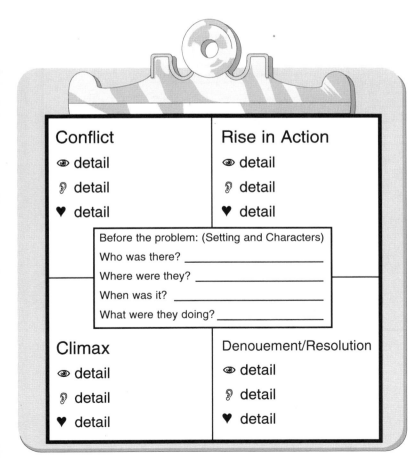

Conflict	Rise in Action
👁 detail	👁 detail
👂 detail	👂 detail
♥ detail	♥ detail

Before the problem: (Setting and Characters)
Who was there? _____
Where were they? _____
When was it? _____
What were they doing? _____

Climax	Denouement/Resolution
👁 detail	👁 detail
👂 detail	👂 detail
♥ detail	♥ detail

The 4□ + 3 stage in a narrative style

Name _____

Directions: Complete the setting, events and ending for the narrative style Four Square. Then add three details per event.

The field trip that went bad

Conflict: _____

_____

👁 _____

👂 _____

❤ _____

Rise in Action: _____

_____

👁 _____

👂 _____

❤ _____

Who was there? _____

Where were they? _____

When was it? _____

What were they doing? _____

Climax:_____

_____

👁 _____

👂 _____

❤ _____

Denouement/Resolution: _____

_____

👁 _____

👂 _____

❤ _____

66

Name _____

Directions: Complete the setting, events and ending for the narrative style Four Square. Then add three details per event.

How I became President

Conflict: _____

_____

 👁 _____

👂 _____

❤ _____

Rise in Action: _____

_____

👁 _____

👂 _____

❤ _____

Who was there? _____

Where were they? _____

When was it? _____

What were they doing? _____

Climax: _____

_____

👁 _____

👂 _____

❤ _____

Denouement/Resolution: _____

_____

👁 _____

👂 _____

❤ _____

4□ + 3 + C

narrative

In the narrative, the use of connecting words and phrases is largely at the discretion of the writer. The words used to connect ideas in a story are called "time connectors," because they are often used to show the lapse of time from one event to the next. Without time connectors, a reader would assume that one event followed immediately after the preceding event. For clarity and stylistic flair, the use of phrases such as "right that minute" or "just then" can help the reader construct the story.

The 4□ + 3 + C stage in a narrative style

Topic

time connector **Conflict**	time connector **Rise in Action**
👁 detail	👁 detail
👂 detail	👂 detail
♥ detail	♥ detail

Who was there? _____

Where were they? _____

When was it? _____

What were they doing? _____

time connector **Climax**	time connector **Denouement/Resolution**
👁 detail	👁 detail
👂 detail	👂 detail
♥ detail	♥ detail

Because of the flexibility of these terms in writing, it would be difficult to color-code them as we did in the informational writing forms. Brainstorming these words and phrases and keeping them close by can help writers seeking the dramatic flair.

TLC10581

Time Connectors

A very incomplete list

First
Next
Then
Last
After that
Immediately
One (second/hour/minute/day/year) later
Soon after that
The next day
Later on
In the beginning
In the end
At (give time)
A long time ago
Long after that
Not long after that
Meanwhile
At the same time
That evening
That morning
That afternoon
Today
Yesterday
Tomorrow
Etc.

4☐ + 3 + C + V

narrative

Vivids make the narrative piece of writing. Narrative writing, driven by action and emotion, relies on the use of specific, descriptive language for explanation. When creating the setting, characters, and events of a narrative, the use of sensory detail, simile and "like what" comparisons, and accurate, precise word choices will bring the readers into the story. Use them liberally!

The 4☐ + 3 + C + V stage in a narrative style

Topic

time connector	time connector
Conflict	**Rise in Action**
👁 detail *vivid*	👁 detail *vivid*
👂 detail *vivid*	👂 detail *vivid*
♥ detail *vivid*	♥ detail *vivid*

Who was there? _____

Where were they? _____

When was it? _____

What were they doing? _____

time connector	time connector
Climax	**Denouement/Resolution**
👁 detail *vivid*	👁 detail *vivid*
👂 detail *vivid*	👂 detail *vivid*
♥ detail *vivid*	♥ detail *vivid*

TLC10581

Name _____

Directions: Complete the narrative Four Square. Remember to start with the setting and events. Then add details and vivids. Time connectors are optional.

What I found in my locker

time connector _____

Conflict: _____

_____

👁 _____

👂 _____

❤ _____

time connector _____

Rise in Action: _____

_____

👁 _____

👂 _____

❤ _____

Who was there? _____

Where were they? _____

When was it? _____

What were they doing? _____

time connector _____

Climax: _____

_____

👁 _____

👂 _____

❤ _____

time connector _____

Denouement/Resolution: _____

_____

👁 _____

👂 _____

❤ _____

Directions: Complete the narrative Four Square. Remember to start with the setting and events. Then add details and vivids. Time connectors are optional.

My teacher became a frog.

time connector _____

Conflict: _____

_____

 _____

_____

_____

time connector _____

Rise in Action: _____

_____

_____

_____

_____

Who was there? _____

Where were they? _____

When was it? _____

What were they doing? _____

time connector _____

Climax: _____

_____

_____

_____

_____

time connector _____

Denouement/Resolution: _____

_____

_____

_____

_____

TLC10581

"Hooks" for Narrative Writing

Engaging the Reader from the Start

The function of the narrative piece is to entertain the reader. In doing so, the writer hopes to grab the reader's interest with the action and characters. One method of attracting reader interest is the use of a hook. The hook at the start of the writing is a device intended to generate curiosity in the reader. Many of the hooks that work with the informational writing styles are effective in the narrative as well. Remember to follow the hook with the foundation, setting and characters of the story.

Helpful Hooks for Narrative Writing

Personal Feeling	*Soccer is not just a game, but an overwhelming obsession. It has taught me so much on the field, but more about being useful in the world.*
Action Lead	*Thwack! The branch snapped as I rode by it. I escaped its backlash, but my pal Terry hadn't been so lucky. I pedaled back to the lump on the ground. It had throttled her right between the eyes.*
Quick Picture Blast	*Runny noses! Scraped knees! So many questions! Doing a babysitting job can be hazardous to your health.*
Exaggeration	*Grandma Louise could make a 300 lb. linebacker tremble with just a passing glance. She could stop an arsenal of Navy Seals with just a flick of her hand. Crocodiles and alligators would swim the other way if she came near. She was no ordinary woman.*

Section 3
Samples of Four Squares and Essays
Informational, Narrative, Persuasive and Descriptive Styles

Use these sample Four Squares and essays as models with your students. You may show them the Four Square and have them use the plan to create an essay. Or provide your students the essay and ask them to build the Four Square. Compare with the Four Square provided. Now it's a reading comprehension activity!

 Additional examples of all types of Four Squares and resulting essays can be found on the enhanced CD.

TLC10581

Informational

One reason

Big bedroom

- room to relax
  big bed
- room for friends
  talk
- closet space
  clothes
  sports equipment

queen-size sleepover

Also

Fireplace

- warm
  like a mitten
- crackling
  like my cereal
- smoky smell
  campfire

gather and snuggle

My home is a special place.

Third

My porch

- screened
  no bugs
- relaxing
  listen to birds
- cool
  evening breezes

morning yogurt

In summary

My home is a special place because it has a big bedroom, a fireplace and a porch.

Informational Essay

Where can you find comfort and all the things you love? At home! My home is a special place. It is special because it has a fireplace, my big bedroom, and my screened porch. It is a wonderful place to live.

One reason my home is special is because of my wonderful, big bedroom. I have a big bed I can relax on. It is a really big, queen-size bed. My parents gave me this new, huge bed for my birthday. I love it because my friends don't have to sleep on the floor when we have sleepovers. We can all hop in the big bed! There is a lot of room in my bedroom for friends, so we can talk privately. My closet has plenty of space for all my clothes and sports equipment, like my basketball and tennis racket.

Also, my fireplace is wonderful. On chilly nights it keeps me warm like a mitten. My family all gathers by the fireplace and we stay warm. My cats like to snuggle on my lap as I sit near the fire. I love the sound of the crackling, it sounds like breakfast cereal! The smoky, woodsy smell reminds me of the days when I go camping.

Third, my home has a terrific porch. The porch is screened, which is lucky for me. I am a bug magnet! My porch is a great place for relaxing. Listening to the birds is a great way to unwind. I love to sit on the porch on mild mornings, eating my yogurt and listening to birds singing. The porch is where I like to be at the end of a long day to enjoy the cool evening breezes.

In summary, my home is special because it has a big bedroom, a fireplace, and a porch. I couldn't imagine living anywhere else.

TLC10581

Narrative

When my cat started talking

Halfway through

Commercial came on

👁 dancing and singing cat on the screen

👂 familiar jingle

❤ I like this. So cute.

During the commercial

Figaro's attitude changed

👁 hair stood up on his back

👂 hissing and growling

❤ worried about him

Who?	My cat, Figaro, and I
What?	Watching television
Where?	Home
When?	Last Saturday evening

Just then

Figaro spoke

👁 walked right up to me

👂 "That food is awful and the dancing cat is a fool."

❤ nearly passed out from the shock

Since that day

We understand each other

👁 a pantry full of the other brand of cat food

👂 only normal cat noises

❤ amazed at the wisdom and power of my cat

TLC10581

Narrative Essay

Last Saturday evening, I was relaxing at home with my adorable orange tabby, Figaro. We were seated together in my favorite chair, Figaro on my lap, watching television.

Halfway through the program, a cat food commercial came on for the brand I always buy. It features a singing and cat, dressed in a coat and tails, dancing on the screen. I knew the familiar jingle, so I started humming along. How cute this is, I thought. I like this commercial.

During the commercial I noticed a change in Figaro. His normally calm attitude disappeared, and he looked pretty upset. He arched his back, and the hair along his spine stood up. Instead of his normal purring and mewing, he was growling and hissing. Where was my beloved kitty? I was so very worried about him.

Just then Figaro spoke. Really, he did! He jumped up onto the back of my chair and walked right up to my ear. Very clearly he said, "That food is awful and the dancing cat is a fool." I nearly passed out from the shock!

Ever since that day, Figaro and I understand each other a whole lot better, but I heard his message. A look in my pantry will find a whole stock of a different brand of cat food. Figaro has never used words again. He's back to making regular cat sounds. I always knew I loved my kitty, but I am still amazed at the wisdom and power of my cat.

TLC10581

Persuasive

One reason
Relaxation
- stress isn't healthy
  heart attacks
- more time for recreation
  watching TV
- catch up on reading
  good book

Detective Whodunnit

Also
Family bonding
- better for children
  being loved
- help with homework
  private tutor
- sharing experiences
  everyday life

Family Garden

The school week should be shortened to three days.

In addition
Less use of school buses
- less pollution
  better for air
- less wear on bus
  save money
- less traffic on roads
  fewer accidents

Bus tires $

Hence

The school week should be shortened to three days so there can be more relaxation and more family bonding, with less use of school buses.

Persuasive Essay

The school week should be shortened to three days. There is a clear need for relaxation and family bonding. Also, this would cause less use of school buses. The evidence supporting this change is clear.

One reason to shorten the school week is the universal need for relaxation. Students and teachers under stress are experiencing a health risk. It could lead to a heart attack. A shorter week would increase the time allowed for recreational activities such as television viewing. Perhaps more students would read if there were a shorter week. There are many good books available. Last Sunday I was reading my way through the Detective Whodunnit books. The mystery was getting more and more interesting, but I had to put the book away and get ready for school. Boy, I wish I had another day for reading and relaxing.

Also, the shorter week would allow time for more family bonding. More quality time is better for children who are so in need of love. Parents can take a role in helping their children with homework; they can act as private home tutors. This shortened week may give   parents the time they need to share the experience of spending every day with their darling children. Doing family projects together would be a way to share experiences. For example, my family usually spends several hours together working in our family garden. While we work in the fresh air, my dad shares his memories of working in the garden with his dad and granddad. These are important times together.

In addition, the shorter week will lessen the use of school buses. Buses are notorious polluters, so giving them two more days off will be better for the air. Less use of the buses means less wear and tear on the vehicles, and this would save taxpayer dollars. In today's economy, we need to make school dollars last. Did you know that one bus tire costs almost $400? Fewer days on the road would be fewer replaced tires. Having fewer buses on the road means less traffic, and there would be fewer accidents.

Hence, the school week should be shortened to three days so there can be more relaxation and more family bonding and less use of school buses. What student or teacher could disagree?

TLC10581

Descriptive

One reason

The grass

- green
  as a frog
- manicured
  perfectly cut
- no weeds
  prohibited

7 men

Also

Memorial Park

- plaques
  delicately engraved
- jerseys
  well-worn
- tattered baseballs
  signed

Retired Numbers

Yankee Stadium is a beautiful place.

Too

The electricity

- always there
  the eyes of the children
- shouting fans
  Tabernacle Choir
- the memory of greatness
  spirits in the air

Standing Ovation

As one can see

Yankee Stadium is a beautiful place because of the grass, Memorial Park and the electricity in the air.

Descriptive Essay

Yankee Stadium is a beautiful place. The beauty can be seen in the grass and Memorial Park, and it can be felt in the electricity in the air. I love to visit there.

One reason it is so beautiful is the grass. It is always frog-green. The lawn is manicured and perfectly cut. Weeds are prohibited from entering. The stadium keeps a staff of seven tending to the grass all year, keeping it a perfect carpet of green in the middle of a city of steel and concrete.

Also, Memorial Park is a special place. One can view the plaques that have been so delicately engraved in remembrance. Some of the most breathtaking plaques show the players who have been honored by having their numbers retired. Some of those players made the Yankees great more than fifty years ago. There are jerseys to view that were well-worn by the greats. They have tattered old baseballs which have priceless signatures.

The electricity in the air is beautiful, too. It is always there, and you can see it in the eyes of the children visiting. The shouting of the fans sounds like the Mormon Tabernacle Choir to the ears of a baseball lover. Once, after a grand slam, the symphony of screaming fans lasted for more than ten minutes. Witnesses swore that the wall of sound was such a mighty roar, it could've been heard in outer space! One can sense the memory of greatness because their spirits live in the air at Yankee Stadium.

As one can see, Yankee Stadium is a beautiful place because of the grass, Memorial Park and the electricity in the air. You should catch a game today.

TLC10581

Section 4
Four Square and Beyond
across the Curriculum

Science

Social Studies

Math

The Arts

4□ in the Language Arts Program

Using Four Square as a Part of the Writing Process

Four Square helps students organize their thoughts. Teaching this method will help students become better writers. The Four Square is an elaborate prewriting activity. It provides much of the material that will be applied in the drafting stage of writing. Four Square helps to eliminate common errors that create a need for rewriting. But Four Square alone is not a writing program.

Students need a variety of activities and approaches to spark their creative writing interest. **Brainstorming** on a topic using a semantic map or sensory web is an activity that can be completed before organizing with the Four Square. Students may have a shared experience to develop their writing skills. Certainly the use of the Four Square does not call for an abandonment of hands-on learning.

After initial brainstorming is underway, the Four Square is a tool for **organizing** that experience. It aligns thoughts and prepares students for a composition.

Drafting follows the organizing step. This is the manuscript created by writers that is full of errors that need fixing, changing and sometimes dumping. It is a natural stage of the writing process and certainly not the last. Unfortunately, this is the stage at which most states make their writing assessment. That is why we need to make the most of organization; it can help limit drafting errors.

Revising and editing follow drafting. This stage encourages proofreading and making structural changes to a piece where clarification or continuity improvements are needed. A proofreading poster is on page 86 for duplication.

During the editing step, students should be encouraged to consider their word choices and sentence structure. In writing, it is desirable to "get the most bang for your buck" and avoid the use of weak language whenever possible.

One way to do this is the use of adverbs and stronger verbs. To develop this sense, a contest can be played using a sentence with a weak or linking verb. Students can be challenged to write as many strong versions of that sentence as possible.

TLC10581

Last year I went to Miami.
Last year I drove to Miami.
Last year I hopped a train to Miami.
Last year I roller bladed to Miami.
Last year I swam to Miami.
Etc.

This is a fun exercise and students can get carried away with it. It also works well with linking verbs.

I am here today.
I stand here today.
I dance here today.
I juggle here today.
I back flip here today.
I hokey-pokey here today.
Etc.

A wall poster that has the five senses plus one formula can be placed as a reminder to students about the vivid language stage. A reproducible poster follows on page 86.

Finally, students need to **publish**. They should occasionally prepare a composition free of errors and written for others to see. Sharing of published work through anthologies or authors' chairs is wonderful for student self-esteem.

Four Square is only one step in this process, but it is a critical one and one often not taught. Given only the sensory web or semantic map, a student will not have a clear direction for composition.

Punctuation!

PUNCTUATION

Do all sentences end with marks?
Is there a reason for each mark I used?
Did I use at least one question or exclamation?

ORGANIZATION

Did I follow my four square?
Do I have good details and vivid words?
Is it neat and organized looking?

PARAGRAPHING

Do I have at least five paragraphs?
Do I have an introduction and a conclusion?
Do I start my sentences differently?

SPELLING

Did I sound out problem words?
Did I check a dictionary?
Have I entered the words in my
    spelling dictionary?

TLC10581

Practical Matters

Tips on Making the Writing Program Work

Supplies

To keep students on task and writing, it is important to have the appropriate hardware readily available. A truckload of pencils and paper is appropriate. It may be cost-effective to use a low-grade newsprint for Four Square preparation and save lined manuscript paper for drafting and rewriting. These supplies should be accessible to students so they can restock without interrupting instruction.

To keep their papers organized, the maintenance of a writing folder is recommended. This folder should have three sections with pockets. The first section in the folder can be used to contain brainstorming activities. The center would hold organizing activities, and the third section would contain compositions. In order to track their work, students should keep a "routing sheet" on the flap of their folder. Each composition has a number, and this number is placed in the upper right-hand corner of every paper generated by the project. The folders should be maintained in a special location in the classroom so they are not lost or destroyed.

Spelling

Spelling is not emphasized throughout Four Square instruction nor through the writing process. Correct spelling and usage becomes critical in the publishing stage of the process. Because this is when the work is prepared for a reading audience, conventional spellings must be used.

Spelling is also an issue when students refuse to write because they cannot spell the words and are not motivated to check a dictionary or reference. In these instances, provide them with a conventional spelling under one condition. They must put the spelling in their personal spelling dictionaries (spiral-bound notebooks work well). As the year progresses, each student will have more of the common words in a personal spelling dictionary and will ask less often.

Conferencing

Practical experience has uncovered that students read almost nothing written on a paper, beyond the grade they achieved. Consequently, it is not a valuable practice to write specific and detailed notes on a paper. The most effective way to aid in student writing growth is the personal conference, even if it is the least time efficient. The trick is how to manage a room of 30-plus students while focusing your attention on one student.

The first requirement is that the others be engaged. Have the class working individually, drafting compositions. This way there should be no inter-student disputes. The conferences can then be called individually. Interruptions will occur, but like anything else, it is a matter of procedure. It is useful to employ an "absolutely no interruptions during conferences" policy. A sign with the message "Not Now" may need to be used during the first few conference sessions. Once students see that you won't be interrupted, they will be less likely to try.

The individual conference is the most valuable lesson a student receives in writing instruction, so don't give up because of management hassles!

TLC10581

Other Uses of 4☐
in the Language Arts Program

Book Review

The Four Square form is an excellent method of preparing the book review paper, starting in even the earliest grades. Using this format is less intimidating when they see it in so many different applications.

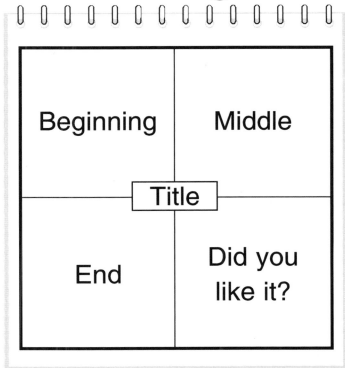

Beginning	Middle
Title	
End	Did you like it?

The Four Square book review

The 4☐ for Reading Comprehension

Four Square can also teach reading comprehension by reading a passage and then building the Four Square that the writer may have used. One effective way to do this uses the students' own writing. An essay that is well-organized and well-written is prepared on a word processor and printed on heavy-duty paper one sentence at a time. These sentences are then cut up and placed in a can. Each student draws a sentence until none are left. The objective is to reconstruct the story. Students must try to find others with similar topics and details. This is a fun and enriching activity. After the story is re-created and read aloud, the original story can be put on chart paper or overhead transparency. The class then tries to re-create the writer's Four Square.

Speeches

Four Square, once mastered, is a fabulous method of preparing notes for speeches or debates. It can contain an entire thesis on one page, including some of the specific details and vivid language intended for use. Once trained in writing from the Four Square, speaking from it will be an easy task.

4□ in the Sciences

Using Four Square as a Study Aid and a Guide to Writing Papers

The Four Square in the expository form adapts well for the sciences. It serves as an excellent way to review or summarize information learned about a specific topic. Using this method to review can provide the student with all the information that is needed for the essay examination, a more authentic form of assessment.

This basic review-style Four Square can be expanded and used as the base for a full-length term paper or research paper.

Certainly the occasion will arise when more than three points are made about a topic. Another "box" can be created for other categories of discourse. Once students understand how each box is developed, they will be able to add another box in abstraction.

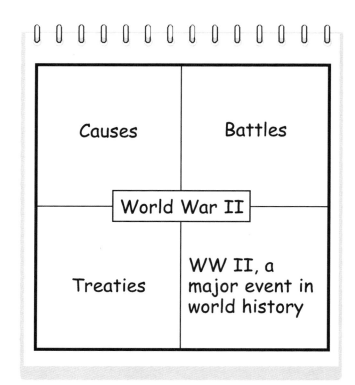

a Four Square used in history

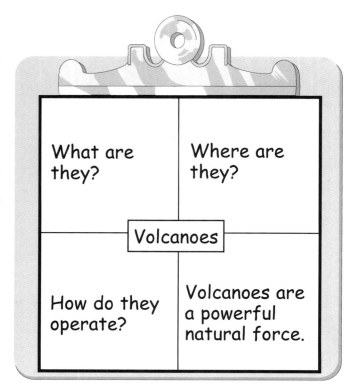

a Four Square used in Earth science

TLC10581

4□ "Within a 4□"

Expanding Subtopics for the Longer Composition

To aid in the development of subtopics for the longer paper, students can use the Four Square to develop each individually. The development of the paper is an easier task if it is viewed as several smaller compositions.

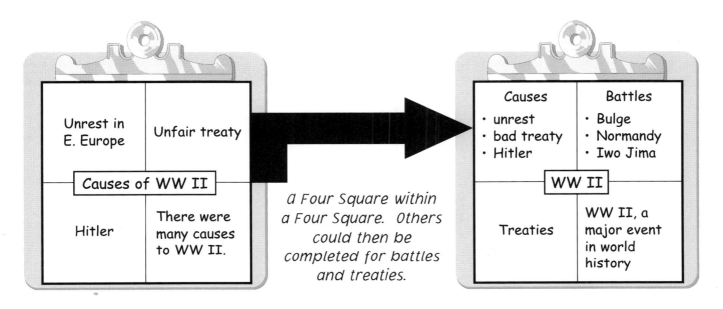

a Four Square within a Four Square. Others could then be completed for battles and treaties.

Four Square is also an excellent tool for comparing information. Completing similar Four Squares on contrasting topics gives a clear picture of the similarities and differences.

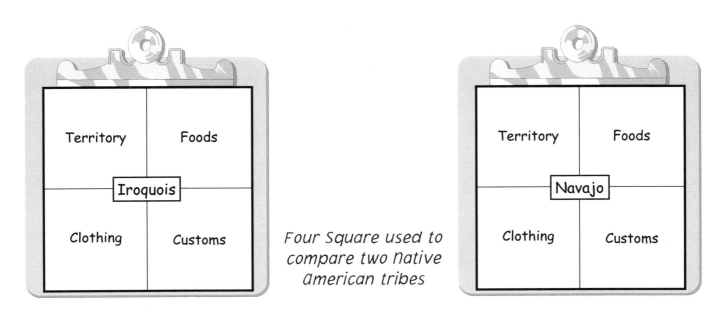

Four Square used to compare two Native American tribes

4□ in Mathematics

Using Four Square to Organize and Solve Word Problems

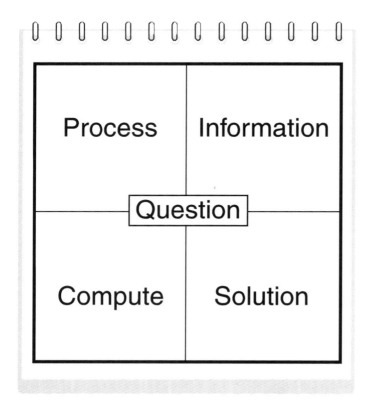

Process	Information
Question	
Compute	Solution

Word problems require the employment of logic and reasoning different from the usual compute and solve drills. These problems require that students develop their own equation and then perform an unnamed operation to find a solution. These steps are not easily completed by the student mathematician.

a Four Square using the P.I.C.S. formula for word problems

The mathematics formula works using a P.I.C.S formula. In the "Process" box the students jot down key words. Certainly lessons will be spent decoding the process for particular question for key words. The "Information" box is for the collection of numerical data. In the "Compute" box the problem is written and computed. The "Solution" box is the area where the student places the answer, along with any proper terminology.

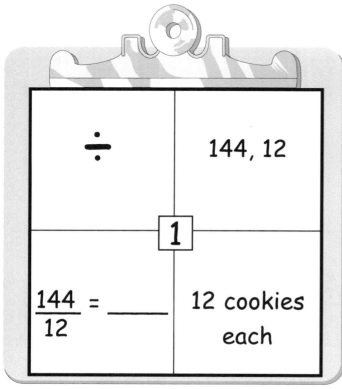

$\div$	144, 12
1	
$\dfrac{144}{12} = $ _____	12 cookies each

1. *Susan had baked 144 cookies during the holidays. She wanted to give some to every girl in her scout troop. There are 12 other girls in her troop. How many cookies will each girl get?*

TLC10581

4☐ in the Arts

Using Four Square for Art and Music Appreciation

A major part of the art and music curricula in the schools is concerned with teaching the various characteristics in a work and helping students discern between artists or composers. With this knowledge and the ability to distinguish styles, it is more likely that a child will become an educated arts consumer.

In music there are some factors that make for an adequate student analysis. If students can describe and compare the factors of form, harmonization, melody, rhythm and orchestration, they can learn to synthesize this information to render a guess as to the composer or musical era.

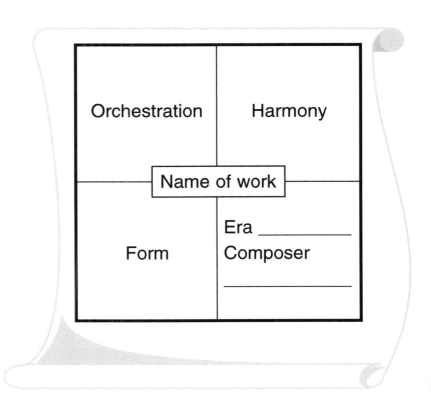

a Four Square for music style analysis

Four Square also works well in the study of program music. Because these works are musical pieces that tell stories without words, students can use the narrative version of the Four Square to re-create and write the story being told.

Interdisciplinary lessons such as these really make the most of class time!

4□ in the Arts

Using Four Square for Art and Music Appreciation

In classroom instruction of the visual arts, a similarly analytical version of the Four Square can be used. While looking at a new work, students can take notes on a Four Square on any number of artistic devices and elements. Box 1 would name the work and box 5 would state the artist and era. Learning about art in an organized fashion will enable students to take a more objective look when viewing something new. Hopefully, they won't rush to a judgment without looking at the traits that display the artist's craft.

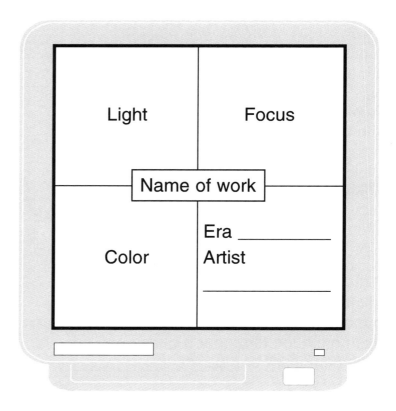

Light	Focus
Name of work	
Color	Era _____ Artist _____

A Four Square for the visual arts style analysis

TLC10581

Preparing for a Writing Assessment

A Lesson in Reading Those Troublesome Writing Prompts

In addition to teaching students the detail and organization that the Four Square helps to build, it is important to provide multiple practice prompts. Often on writing assessments, students are faced with prompts that are new and unfamiliar. Only through experience in working with writing prompts can we help students face this situation with confidence. In deciphering the topic for the Four Square middle box, we can help our students to TAP out the prompt. TAP is a handy acronym that asks students to seek out the topic, audience, and purpose of the writing.

T.A.P. Out Those Prompts

T opic (goes in your four square center)

A udience (information, description, convincing or a story)

P urpose (expository, descriptive, persuasive or narrative)

Expository	Persuasive	Descriptive	Narrative
Inform	Convince	Describe	Story
Tell steps	Persuade	Senses	Events
Explain			"Happens"
Examples			
Reasons			

T.A.P Those Prompts

Directions: Read each prompt. Remember the three parts to the prompt. Be sure to underline the "what to write" part. Then complete the topic, audience and purpose for each prompt.

1. Occasionally we find ourselves in a dangerous situation. Think about a time when you had a narrow escape from danger. Tell a story about the experience.

   Topic: (Center Box) _____

   Audience: (Information, Description, Convincing or Story) _____

   Purpose: (Expository, Descriptive, Persuasive or Narrative) _____

2. Your school is going to get a new mascot; they need to choose an animal. Think about which animal you would like for the school mascot. Write to convince your principal to choose your mascot.

   Topic: (Center Box) _____

   Audience: (Information, Description, Convincing or Story) _____

   Purpose: (Expository, Descriptive, Persuasive or Narrative) _____

3. Everyone has a special place in his or her home. Where is your special place? Describe the spot in your home that is your favorite.

   Topic: (Center Box) _____

   Audience: (Information, Description, Convincing or Story) _____

   Purpose: (Expository, Descriptive, Persuasive or Narrative) _____

4. Children often daydream or fantasize about what they would like their lives to be when they become adults. Hard work and planning can make a dream come true. Think about your goals for the future. Explain to your reader what steps you will take to reach those goals.

   Topic: (Center Box) _____

   Audience: (Information, Description, Convincing or Story) _____

   Purpose: (Expository, Descriptive, Persuasive or Narrative) _____

T.A.P Those Prompts Answer Key

Directions: Read each prompt. Remember the three parts to the prompt. Be sure to underline the "what to write" part. Then complete the topic, audience and purpose for each prompt.

1. Occasionally we find ourselves in a dangerous situation. Think about a time when you had a narrow escape from danger. Tell a story about the experience.

    Topic: (Center Box) __My narrow escape from danger__

    Audience: (Information, Description, Convincing or Story) __Story__

    Purpose: (Expository, Descriptive, Persuasive or Narrative) __Narrative__

2. Your school is going to get a new mascot; they need to choose an animal. Think about which animal you would like for the school mascot. Write to convince your principal to choose your mascot.

    Topic: (Center Box) __I want a guinea pig for our mascot.__

    Audience: (Information, Description, Convincing or Story) __Convincing__

    Purpose: (Expository, Descriptive, Persuasive or Narrative) __Persuasive__

3. Everyone has a special place in his or her home. Where is your special place? Describe the spot in your home that is your favorite.

    Topic: (Center Box) __My porch__

    Audience: (Information, Description, Convincing or Story) __Description__

    Purpose: (Expository, Descriptive, Persuasive or Narrative) __Descriptive__

4. Children often daydream or fantasize about what they would like their lives to be when they become adults. Hard work and planning can make a dream come true. Think about your goals for the future. Explain to your reader what steps you will take to reach those goals.

    Topic: (Center Box) __I want to be a brain surgeon.__

    Audience: (Information, Description, Convincing or Story) __Information__

    Purpose: (Expository, Descriptive, Persuasive or Narrative) __Expository__

Name _____

T.A.P Those Prompts

Directions: Read each prompt. Remember the three parts to the prompt. Be sure to underline the "what to write" part. Then complete the topic, audience and purpose for each prompt.

1. The Fountain of Youth is an important historical spot. Imagine that you discovered the Fountain of Youth. Explain how you felt and what happened.

   Topic: (Center Box) _____

   Audience: (Information, Description, Convincing or Story) _____

   Purpose: (Expository, Descriptive, Persuasive or Narrative) _____

2. Sometimes when things are lost we must put an ad in a newspaper to help find it. Think about your book bag or knapsack. Describe it for the newspaper ad.

   Topic: (Center Box) _____

   Audience: (Information, Description, Convincing or Story) _____

   Purpose: (Expository, Descriptive, Persuasive or Narrative) _____

3. You work hard around your house doing many chores. You keep up your good grades. Think about all the things you do to please your parents. Write to persuade them to give you a bigger allowance.

   Topic: (Center Box) _____

   Audience: (Information, Description, Convincing or Story) _____

   Purpose: (Expository, Descriptive, Persuasive or Narrative) _____

4. "A dog is a man's best friend" is an old expression. Think of the ways a dog or other pet is a friend to a particular person. Tell your reader the ways the dog or other pet helps this person. Give reasons and examples.

   Topic: (Center Box) _____

   Audience: (Information, Description, Convincing or Story) _____

   Purpose: (Expository, Descriptive, Persuasive or Narrative) _____

TLC10581

T.A.P Those Prompts Answer Key

Directions: Read each prompt. Remember the three parts to the prompt. Be sure to underline the "what to write" part. Then complete the topic, audience and purpose for each prompt.

1. The Fountain of Youth is an important historical spot. Imagine that you discovered the Fountain of Youth. Explain how you felt and what happened.

   Topic: (Center Box) __When I discovered the Fountain of Youth__

   Audience: (Information, Description, Convincing or Story) __Story__

   Purpose: (Expository, Descriptive, Persuasive or Narrative) __Narrative__

2. Sometimes when things are lost we must put an ad in a newspaper to help find it. Think about your book bag or knapsack. Describe it for the newspaper ad.

   Topic: (Center Box) __My book bag__

   Audience: (Information, Description, Convincing or Story) __Description__

   Purpose: (Expository, Descriptive, Persuasive or Narrative) __Descriptive__

3. You work hard around your house doing many chores. You keep up your good grades. Think about all the things you do to please your parents. Write to persuade them to give you a bigger allowance.

   Topic: (Center Box) __I should get a bigger allowance.__

   Audience: (Information, Description, Convincing or Story) __Convincing__

   Purpose: (Expository, Descriptive, Persuasive or Narrative) __Persuasive__

4. "A dog is a man's best friend" is an old expression. Think of the ways a dog or other pet is a friend to a particular person. Tell your reader the ways the dog or other pet helps this person. Give reasons and examples.

   Topic: (Center Box) __My dog helps me.__

   Audience: (Information, Description, Convincing or Story) __Information__

   Purpose: (Expository, Descriptive, Persuasive or Narrative) __Expository__

Section 5
Practice Prompts
Expository, Narrative, Persuasive and Descriptive Styles

Think It!

Plan It!

Write It!

Do It!

TLC10581

Directions: Read the prompt. Identify the "Who cares?" "Brain activation" and "What to write" parts. Underline the "What to write" part.

You get your first job delivering newspapers. One of the houses on your route is very special. Write a story about your adventures at the house.

Topic: (Center of your 4☐) _____

_____

Audience: (Circle one.)

| Information | Description | Convincing | Story |

Purpose: (Circle one.)

| Expository | Persuasive | Descriptive | Narrative |

Directions:
Complete a
4☐ + 3 + C + V + E

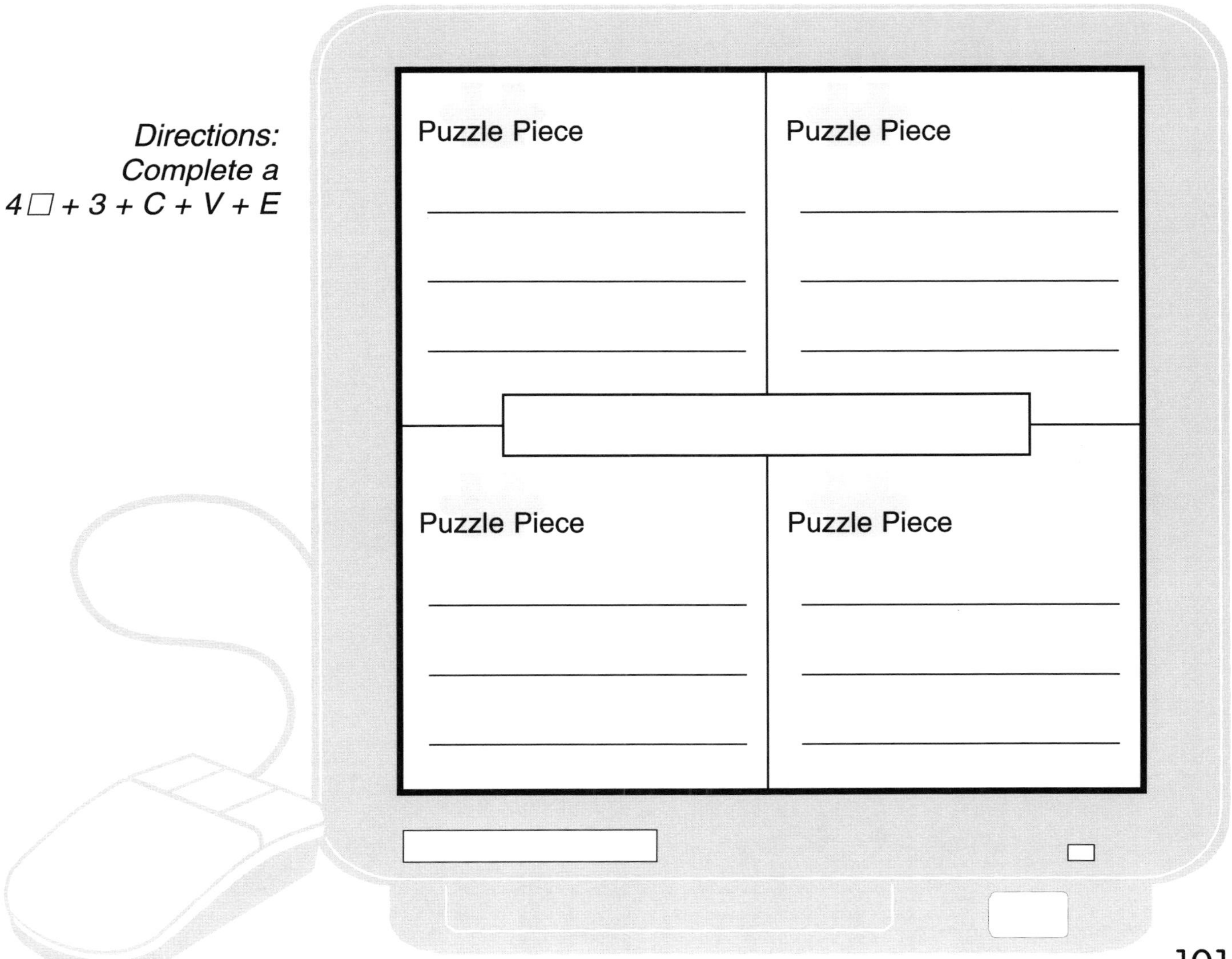

Puzzle Piece
_____
_____
_____

Puzzle Piece
_____
_____
_____

Puzzle Piece
_____
_____
_____

Puzzle Piece
_____
_____
_____

Directions: Write your story!

Paragraph 1

_____

_____

_____

_____

Paragraph 2

_____

_____

_____

_____

Paragraph 3

_____

_____

_____

_____

Paragraph 4

_____

_____

_____

_____

Paragraph 5

_____

_____

_____

_____

Did you indent each paragraph (five times)?
Do you have your capitals and periods?
Did you write from margin to margin?

Directions: Read the prompt. Identify the "Who cares?" "Brain activation" and "What to write" parts. Underline the "What to write" part.

A local handyman is looking for someone to work for an hour after school to clean his shop and help with some easy chores. Persuade the handyman that you are the best person for this job.

Topic: (Center of your 4☐) _____

_____

Audience: (Circle one.)

Information   Description   Convincing   Story

Purpose: (Circle one.)

Expository   Persuasive   Descriptive   Narrative

Directions:
Complete a
4☐ + 3 + C + V + E

Puzzle Piece	Puzzle Piece
_____	_____
_____	_____
_____	_____
Puzzle Piece	Puzzle Piece
_____	_____
_____	_____
_____	_____

Directions: Write your story!

Paragraph 1

_____

_____

_____

_____

_____

Paragraph 2

_____

_____

_____

_____

Paragraph 3

_____

_____

_____

_____

Paragraph 4

_____

_____

_____

_____

Paragraph 5

_____

_____

_____

_____

Did you indent each paragraph (five times)?
Do you have your capitals and periods?
Did you write from margin to margin?

TLC10581

Directions: Read the prompt. Identify the "Who cares?" "Brain activation" and "What to write" parts. Underline the "What to write" part.

You are planning a trip around the world. You must choose one way to travel. Think about all the different types of transportation. Which would you choose? Explain why.

Topic: (Center of your 4☐) _____

_____

Audience: (Circle one.)

Information   Description   Convincing   Story

Purpose: (Circle one.)

Expository   Persuasive   Descriptive   Narrative

Directions:
Complete a
4☐ + 3 + C + V + E

Puzzle Piece	Puzzle Piece
_____	_____
_____	_____
_____	_____
Puzzle Piece	Puzzle Piece
_____	_____
_____	_____
_____	_____

Directions: Write your story!

Paragraph 1

_____

_____

_____

_____

Paragraph 2

_____

_____

_____

_____

Paragraph 3

_____

_____

_____

_____

TLC10581

Paragraph 4

_____

_____

_____

_____

Paragraph 5

_____

_____

_____

_____

Did you indent each paragraph (five times)?
Do you have your capitals and periods?
Did you write from margin to margin?

Directions: Read the prompt. Identify the "Who cares?" "Brain activation" and "What to write" parts. Underline the "What to write" part.

Every teacher has his or her own way of decorating a classroom. Think about the things your teacher has used to decorate. Describe your classroom for your reader. Be sure to include many details.

Topic: (Center of your 4☐) _____

_____

Audience: (Circle one.)

Information   Description   Convincing   Story

Purpose: (Circle one.)

Expository   Persuasive   Descriptive   Narrative

Directions: Complete a 4☐ + 3 + C + V + E

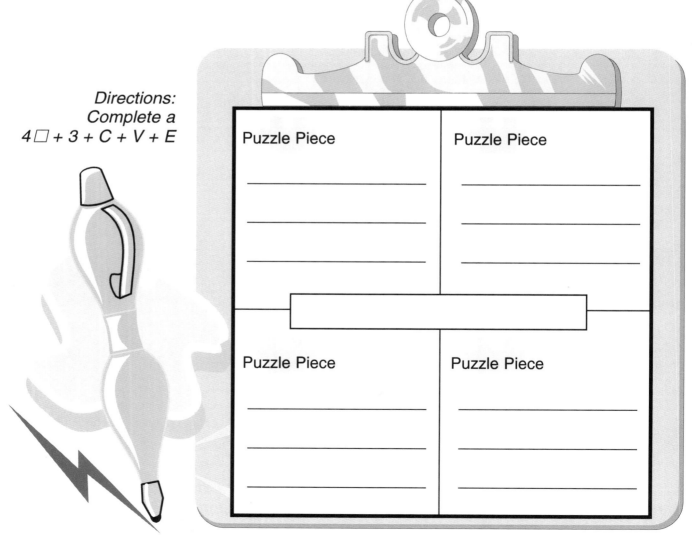

Puzzle Piece

_____
_____
_____

Puzzle Piece

_____
_____
_____

Puzzle Piece

_____
_____
_____

Puzzle Piece

_____
_____
_____

Name _____

Directions: Write your story!

Paragraph 1

_____

_____

_____

_____

Paragraph 2

_____

_____

_____

_____

Paragraph 3

_____

_____

_____

_____

Paragraph 4

_____

_____

_____

_____

_____

Paragraph 5

_____

_____

_____

_____

_____

Did you indent each paragraph (five times)?
Do you have your capitals and periods?
Did you write from margin to margin?

TLC10581